Praise for

The God Who Blesses

When working alongside youth and volunteers, I frequently find myself using the word *bless*—but what do I really mean? In his approachable work, Dr. Jackson took me on a journey to find a more accurate and thoughtful understanding and application of *blessing*, one that both protects me from a superstitious, compulsive, or guilt-based use, and brings me closer to a reverent, flourishing, and dynamic praxis. In doing so, he has allowed me to more fully embrace God's creativity and provision, prompting me to ask what I can do in response and how I can share this with others in my life—for which I am deeply grateful.

—**Erik Brucker**, Area Director, Young Life International, Central London, England

***

The words *bless* and *blessings* roll easily off our tongues. But how many of us truly understand their rich meanings? Gordon Jackson leads us on a trail of discovery through the Bible and places us in real life situations where we can apply what we have learnt. Here is a much needed, readable book certain to enrich the lives of ordinary Christians.

—**Malcolm de Kock**, Pastor Emeritus, Uniting Presbyterian Church in Southern Africa

***

Gordon Jackson's short book on *The God Who Blesses* is a treasure. He explores the deep meanings of blessing in the Bible and draws out their practical significance today. He addresses different misconceptions about God's blessing (such as the "prosperity Gospel") and cautions against trivialized and self-serving notions about blessings. In fifty

short and pithy chapters, *The God Who Blesses* offers much food for reflection, and provocative material for small-group study.
—**Leslie P. Fairfield**, Professor Emeritus of Church History, Trinity School for Ministry, Ambridge, PA.

***

Gordon Jackson brings sharp clarity and depth to the vastly misused concept of "blessing" in our world today, and invites us on a delightful journey into a profoundly important facet of God's love for us in very real and tangible ways.
—**Randy Larsen**, Recruitment and Mobilization, Engineering Ministries International

***

Gordon Jackson's reflections on blessings from God and the state of blessedness are thoughtful, challenging and encouraging. His wit and wisdom come through in this delightful commentary, providing thoughtful insights into this often-over-looked aspect of the journey of Christian faith. I wholeheartedly recommend this book!
—**Krisi Sonneland**, Spiritual Director & Staff Chaplain, Camp Spalding, Newport, WA

***

The God Who Blesses presents refreshing reflections and insights on "blessings." Gordon Jackson invites readers into a deeper understanding of this concept by unpacking the nuanced meanings of the word and gently contrasting the popular of these meanings against the light of Scripture. A must read!
—**Josh Vinton**, Executive Director, Village Schools International

The God Who Blesses

50 Reflections on Blessings and Blessedness

Gordon S. Jackson

Published by KHARIS PUBLISHING, imprint of KHARIS MEDIA LLC.

Copyright © 2022 Gordon S. Jackson

ISBN-13: 978-1-63746-145-7

ISBN-10: 1-63746-145-3

Library of Congress Control Number: 2022941632

Scripture taken from THE HOLY BIBLE, NEW INTERNATIONAL VERSION ®. Copyright© 1973, 1978, 1984, 2011 by Biblica, Inc.™. Used by permission of Zondervan

All KHARIS PUBLISHING products are available at special quantity discounts for bulk purchase for sales promotions, premiums, fund-raising, and educational needs. For details, contact:

Kharis Media LLC

Tel: 1-479-599-8657

support@kharispublishing.com

www.kharispublishing.com

Christ's last act before His ascension was to bless His disciples....

—Andrew Davison[1]

---

[1] Andrew Davison, *Blessing*, p. 3.

Contents

PART 5: Concluding Matters

PART 1

The Basics

Introduction

When our children were young, we'd tuck them in at bedtime, read them a Bible story, and say a prayer we had improvised for them: "God bless Sarah, and keep her safe and well and happy." And "God bless Matthew and keep him safe and well and happy."

At the time, I now realize, I gave little thought to what lay behind our simple "God bless" prayers. What were the theological underpinnings of these blessings? What exactly were our prayers seeking?

It's with some embarrassment that I realize my thinking was a far cry from that of Annie Dillard's, in her caution to Christians about their glib understanding of worship. In *Teaching a Stone to Talk*, she slapped Christians on the side of the head for their cavalier treatment of worship. Instead of expecting a Sunday morning service to be a genial, uneventful way to spend part of the weekend, she asked: "Does anyone have the foggiest idea what sort of power we [Christians] so blithely invoke?" She answered her question by asserting that "It is madness to wear ladies' straw hats and velvet hats to church; we should all be wearing crash helmets. Ushers should issue life preservers and signal flares; they should lash us to our pews."[2]

In retrospect, I realize I brought none of that same sense of awe and reverence to our simple prayer. Nor did I to my thinking about the words *bless*, *blessing*, and *blessed*. When we talk about a God who delights in pouring out on His people something we term blessings, we should hang our heads in shame over how often we have stripped the concept of its power.

---

[2] Annie Dillard, *Teaching a Stone to Talk*, p. 58.

Then there's the other side of the coin: We bless people when they sneeze. We'll say in frustration, "Where did I leave my blessed keys?" We'll say "Bless you" as a synonym for "thanks" when our spouse cleans up after the cat puked on the rug. Fortunately, our prayers over our children, simple though they were, were at least God-focused and genuine petitions for our children's well-being. It wasn't as if we had asked God to bless our new deep fryer or three-hole punch.

These casual blessings abound, it seems. And in the great scheme of things, probably no harm results from these informal, idiomatic uses of the word. But there remains a danger, a risk of trivializing God's goodness to us and diminishing what should be our welcome duty: to "Praise God from whom all blessings flow," as Thomas Ken (1637-1722) put it centuries ago.

The words *bless*, *blessed*, and *blessings* are slippery creatures. They take on multiple meanings. With that range of meanings comes the continuum of everything from the vague email sign-off of "Blessings" to the holy, majestic and awe-filled recognition that we serve a God who is indeed the One from whom all blessings flow.

So what does all this mean, and why does it merit a book-length evaluation? Three reasons. First, there's a considerable amount of theology embedded in the verb *to bless*, in the noun *blessing*, and in the adjective *blessed*. Ironically, though, despite this ripe area of study, "[N]either systematic nor biblical theologians have shown much interest in blessing...."[3] Those of us who are not trained theologians ought to pay some attention to what Scripture says about these concepts, and the main themes that theologians have identified as worthy of attention.

Second, those of us who are serious about our faith owe it to ourselves to take a closer look at a concept (or set of concepts: *bless/blessing/blessed*) that we bandy about with seemingly little thought to what we're saying. We may need a corrective to the casualness we bring to our understanding of this threefold concept. In the book of James, we read, "Out of the same mouth come praise and cursing. My

---

[3] Claus Westermann, *Blessing: In the Bible and the Life of the Church*, p. xv.

brothers and sisters, this should not be."[4] So too with our use of the concept of blessings. On the one hand, we'll say in worship things like "Bless the Lord O my soul"—and later that day, use a phrase like, "Well bless my cotton socks." Really? Blessing socks? Maybe a sock-blessing is an innocent enough invocation. But what if it isn't? What if, to use James' words, "this should not be"? It is worth asking the question.

Finally, as with so much in our faith, the closer we look at a particular concept, the more we discover. As we keep turning a multifaceted diamond, we see new beauty and begin to grasp what a masterpiece a jeweler has crafted. So too with the concept of blessing: Our possible insights into God's grace of course go beyond our appreciation of even the most spectacular jewel, whose features are finite. Not so with the infinite dimensions of God's character and works, one aspect of which is an overflowing readiness to bless us, His people.

Why God chooses to bless us is a mystery that we mortals cannot answer; all we can do is embrace these blessings with gratitude. But there are a host of other blessing-related questions that we can at least ask, even if they are ultimately just as unanswerable. To whet your appetite, here are ten that we'll explore, among others:

- What do we mean by *bless, blessing* and *blessed*?
- What is the theology behind blessing? (What does Scripture have to say about this?)
- On what authority does one get to do the blessing? (Does a blessing flow from a greater to lesser power?)
- What does a state of blessedness look like?
- Who or what merits a blessing? (Is "Bless this ship and all who sail on her" OK but not "Please bless my car's new muffler"?)

---

[4] James 3:10.

- Can we imagine Jesus giving one of the disciples a heartfelt "Bless you" after a sneeze? If not, why not?

- What difference does a blessing actually make? (If the priest or pastor is blessing the children who come to the altar during the Eucharist, and your toddler stays sleeping soundly in the pew, has she lost out? If so, how?)

- Is a blessing in disguise really a blessing?

- Can we demand a blessing from God?

- And what's the Mount of Blessings vs the Mount of Cursings all about?

A few technical and personal things before we begin. All Scripture references are from the *New International Version* of the Bible, except where noted otherwise. Then there is the issue of inclusive language. Some quotes use *man, mankind* and so on when referring to people in general. These quotes reflect earlier usage which characterizes contemporary English less and less. In keeping with this volume's commitment to present all sources as accurately as possible, I have included these entries with their original wording. The use of masculine pronouns to refer to God is done with due deference to concerns about inclusive language. Their use is not to assert that God is masculine. Where possible, attempts have been made to avoid masculine pronouns. But they have been included rather than resort to the heavy-handed artificiality of writing things like "We seek to know who God is, how God deals with us, and what God Godself wants to characterize our life together as God's people." Elsewhere, quoted material using these pronouns is left unchanged, out of the need to present these sources accurately.

The reflections that follow are simply that: a layman's reflections on this concept of blessings. This is not an attempt at a systematic theological analysis of the concept, for which I am supremely unqualified. For an in-depth theological exploration of the topic, check out Andrew Davison's *Blessing* and Claus Westermann's *Blessing: In the Bible and in the Church.*

Instead, what follows is a non-theologian's effort to explore a concept that is so familiar to us that we've lost sight of much of its richness. The reflections are in no particular order. I encourage you though to read the first two entries: on God's readiness to bless and a definition of blessing so that we will be on the same page as you proceed. Thereafter, feel free to dip into the entries at random. There's no sequence of topics or careful argument that you need to follow. References to other entries are in bold.

However you approach the material, I invite you to do so with an unrelenting awareness of God's readiness to bless us. You're further invited to embrace for yourself the *Anglican Book of Common Prayer's* statement in the morning prayer for the clergy and the people, "Pour upon them the continual dew of thy blessing."

1

The God Who Blesses

Reflecting on the expansive nature of God's grace, theologian and philosopher Peter Kreeft says, "God created freely. No beings are necessary except God. Nothing else has to be; everything else is 'contingent.' Everything that was not created (like a green tiger) is a might-have-been, and everything that was created (like an orange tiger) is a might-not-have-been. It is a sheer gift, a sheer grace."[5]

As we bring this closer to home, to you and me, we ought to grasp that God's lavish creativity extends to the grace shown in creating each one of us. Our very existence is the most personal blessing we can enjoy. To use Kreeft's wording, each of us is a "might-not-have-been" feature of God's creation. If you hadn't overcome the astonishing odds of a particular sperm fertilizing a particular egg, your parents would not have had *you*—but a sibling quite different from you in countless ways.

It's important to note that God blesses on His terms, as He sees fit. Thomas à Kempis wrote in the medieval period, "God has the right to send blessings and comfort when he wishes, as much as he wishes, to whom he wishes, just as he pleases and no more."[6] However God does so, it's plain that He is a God of blessing. It apparently gives Him great joy to make us—not only you and me but quite literally billions of

---

[5] Peter Kreeft, *Angels and Demons*, p. 37.
[6] Thomas à Kempis, *The Imitation of Christ*, translated by Betty Knott, p. 121.

us. Blessing us is in His self-chosen job description; that's what He *does*. It's in His nature and character to want to give us good things. As Watchman Nee puts it, "God is so wealthy that His chief delight is to give."[7]

Elsewhere we'll look at the reasons we ignore or reject His blessings. But for now, we need to grasp this simple point: Our maker cannot help showering us with blessings and keeps on doing so even though at times we humans inexplicably take out our umbrellas to avoid them.

---

[7] Watchman Nee, *Sit, Walk, Stand*, p. 20.

2

Beyond Unicorns: *Blessing* Defined

Y ou can be excused for not thinking about unicorns if you're asked to define the word *blessing*. Yet that's the collective noun for these mythical beasts. More likely, you're focused on an equally intangible but far more profound concept, one that embodies nine key features. After describing these features, we'll offer a definition of blessing that we'll rely on in the rest of this book.

But before we begin, we should note that *bless*, *blessing* and *blessedness* have different implications. It's not easy to draw a fine line between these three tightly linked concepts. Nevertheless, there are distinctions between their meanings. To *bless* entails a specific action or statement, seeking a God-derived good for the recipient of the blessing—a point we'll explore presently. To bless is sharply focused, such as the blessing that comes at the end of worship when the pastor or priest dismisses the congregation. It can be limited in time or ongoing, such as God blessing Abraham and Sarah with their promised son, Isaac. Usually, the recipients are aware that they have been blessed in this particular way.

Blessing, however, can be more general, referring to aspects of **Shalom** in our lives that we may not even be aware of.[8] Yes, we may be conscious of a blessing (a recovery from a near-fatal bout of

---

[8] We will discuss the link between blessings and Shalom later. For now we'll briefly define *Shalom* as the ideal state that God envisions for his people, one marked by "flourishing, wholeness, completeness, harmony, prosperity and tranquility."

COVID), but we may not. (If we think about it, it's a blessing that our carotid artery isn't failing us today.) Our usage of blessing can become so general that anything and everything good is defined that way. Think for instance of the refrain in the hymn, "We plow the fields and scatter, the good seed on the land." It goes:

All good gifts around us are sent from heav'n above.
We thank you, God, we thank you, God, for all your love.

That is, "all good gifts" include many we don't recognize.

Then, *blessedness* is distinguished by its passive nature. It's a condition in which people find themselves, thanks to an action that God or another person has undertaken on God's behalf. Unlike the active verb, to bless, *blessedness* is an outcome. If I am blessed or in a state of blessedness, I have done nothing to deserve it.

We also need to distinguish between two types of blessing: what we'll term *hallowed blessings*, which have their origin in God, and *colloquial* or informal ones, which most likely do not. The former are our present focus but we'll come back to the colloquial ones later.

When we're talking about hallowed or real or serious blessings, as we will most of the time, here's what we have in mind:

<u>A blessing calls for or seeks to initiate something good</u>: Typically, we're talking about good health, a long life, safety, and prosperity (however one defines that). It may include a desire to have children. But the priorities of the person or persons being blessed may change over time and vary by culture. In a pastoral society, you might include in a blessing a prayer that flocks will be healthy and fruitful.

In today's Western societies, you wouldn't necessarily assume that a pair of newlyweds wanted a large family, something taken for granted just a few generations ago. So a wedding blessing that in the past would have generated a laugh may not go down well today: "May your marriage be blessed with the wisdom of Solomon, the patience of Job, and the children of Israel." In brief, a blessing speaks to what is assumed to be desirable and a priority for the recipient of the blessing.

<u>A blessing is ultimately derived from or rooted in God</u>: Andrew Davison writes that "A blessing recognizes the goodness of God's creation. This links blessing to a central task of Christian discipleship,

namely learning to see the world from a Christian perspective."[9] From this perspective, then, a blessing is something calling for God's grace to be activated. It's as if we're saying, "God, would You please make good things happen for this person, persons or even an event or thing." In other words, we're talking about moving the state of things one step closer to **Shalom**, the condition of things as God would have them be.

When we hear a blessing, whether it's hallowed or colloquial, we need to remember that there's an assumption underlying the blessing, possibly unspoken but nevertheless implicit. If God isn't explicitly identified as the force behind the blessing, we need to remind ourselves that whatever good will arise from the blessing ultimately derives from God, not you or me. As Paul told the Ephesians, "Every good and perfect gift is from above, coming down from the Father of the heavenly lights...."[10]

Bless, Blessing and *Blessedness* have a wide range of synonyms: Just as blessing can cover a wide range of concepts, so does the inherent meaning of the word. Its meanings include *approve, consecrate, exalt, hallow, sanctify*, and *thank*. Add to this list the word *benison*, which has been in English since the thirteenth century. It is derived from the Latin *benedicere*, meaning *to bless*. The state of being blessed, or blessedness, is sometimes translated in our Bibles as *happiness*, as in *The Living Bible*.

Others, though, see *happiness* as inadequate for capturing the intent of **The Beatitudes**, for example. One commentator notes that "[Thomas] Carlyle insists that blessedness is the better word [than *happiness*], lest *happiness* be confused with a mere hedonism...."[11] John Stott adds another insight when he agrees that *happy* is an inadequate translation of *makarios,* the Greek word typically used for *blessing*. That's because *happiness* is a subjective state, whereas Jesus is talking about an objective state in which His followers *are* already blessed.[12]

A synonym to be avoided altogether is *lucky*, as in "I was so lucky to get the Schwanzenberger account on my first sales call." Or, "We've

---

[9] Andrew Davison, *Blessing*, p. 6.
[10] James 1:17.
[11] *The Interpreter's Bible*, Vol. 7, p 279.
[12] John Stott, *The Message of the Sermon on the Mount*, p. 33.

been so lucky in avoiding COVID." The concept of luck butts head-on with the idea of God's role in your life. Christians who've thought things through realize that they live by *grace*—God's grace—not *luck*, either because of His active blessing in some aspect of our life or because His permissive will has allowed something bad to occur. But *luck*? Not so.

A blessing is closely correlated with, but different from, the concept of grace: Paragraph 2 above indicated that a blessing arises from God's grace. Someone said that "Grace is described as receiving from God what we *do not* deserve, and mercy as not receiving from God what we *do* deserve."[13] Likewise, we don't *deserve* God's blessings; they flow from His grace. They are not an entitlement.

But grace differs from blessings in three ways. First, blessings arise from God's grace, or as a petition for God's grace, in a given setting. It's not the other way round; blessings don't result in grace. Second, grace is overarching and all-encompassing, whereas blessings are focused and targeted. And third, God's grace is central to salvation. As Van Harvey puts it, "Grace is perhaps the most crucial concept in Christian theology because it refers to the free and unmerited act through which God restores His estranged creatures to Himself."[14] We are saved by grace, not by blessings; they are what we could call a by-product, or a subset, of God's overarching grace.

Blessing is not synonymous with salvation. Claus Westermann says that "...in the Old Testament the concept 'salvation' includes both blessing and deliverance, that is, God's activity of blessing and of rescuing His people."[15] He explains that there is a difference between being *saved* or *delivered*, on the one hand, and being *blessed*, on the other. Nevertheless, he says, "From the beginning to the end of the biblical story, God's two ways of dealing with mankind—deliverance and blessing—are found together."[16]

He adds that distinguishing between God's saving and blessing roles is important because it points to different aspects of God's

---

[13] Source unknown.
[14] Van Harvey, *A Handbook of Theological Terms*, p. 108.
[15] Claus Westermann, *Blessing: In the Bible and the Life of the Church*, pp. xv-xvi.
[16] Claus Westermann, *Blessing: In the Bible and the Life of the Church*, pp. 3-4.

dealings with humankind. "The God who saves is the one who comes; the one who blesses is the one who is present..."[17] Our definition, then, focuses only on the blessing role that God plays; He is present with us, eager to bring about good in our daily lives. Of course, being saved is in itself a blessing. But the act of blessing is secondary to God's acts of salvation. Blessings subsequent to salvation are "God's gravy," as it were: manifestations of His lavish love for us. It's as if God has rescued us from a shipwreck, an act of great blessing in itself. Now, in addition, He is giving us warm blankets, hot chocolate, and a phone to call home and tell our family that we're safe.

A blessing is usually bestowed by a greater power or agency to a lesser, but not always: We normally think of God blessing people; a priest or pastor blessing a congregation or individuals; or someone at a wedding reception (perhaps a parent) blessing his or her daughter and the marriage. The direction is from superior to lesser. This is certainly the case when we're talking about wishing good things for the recipient.

Another kind of blessing though reverses the flow; when we think of blessing as praise or thanks. For example, the psalmist says: "Bless the Lord, O my soul: and all that is within me, bless His holy name."[18] While we can bless God in the sense of praising Him, we can't bless Him in the sense of making things better for Him.

A blessing can be directed toward things and occasions as well as people: You've no doubt heard about the formal blessing that may be given at the launch of a new ship or the blessing of a house. We'll look at this topic at greater length, in the entry **God Bless This Ship**. Blessings can also be associated with time. Davison notes that God blesses the seventh day by proclaiming it holy, adding: "Time, like people, places and things, can be holy,"[19]

The term *blessing* is used both formally and casually: As we saw in the **Introduction**, the way we use the idea of blessing varies widely. For want of better terms, we'll distinguish between *hallowed* or real

---

[17] Claus Westermann, *Blessing: In the Bible and the Life of the Church*, p. 8.
[18] Psalm 103:1 (*King James Version*).
[19] Andrew Davison, *Blessing*, p. 188.

blessings, ones to be taken seriously, and those that are casual or merely *colloquial*. There's a vast gap between saying "bless you!" after a sneeze, and how we "bless God" as we praise Him, or a minister blessing a congregation at the end of a service.

A blessing is far more than a wish or a hope: Blessings are unlike a wish your six-year-old makes as she blows out the candles on her birthday cake. A wish is just that, something we'd like to come true ("I wish I'd win the lottery/I wish the neighbor's dog would shut up/I wish our mayor would get those potholes fixed.") But we bring a range of feelings to those wishes, from a wistful optimism that maybe some good will come my way, to a resignation that accepts my fate. (You know you won't win the lottery, the dog will keep barking, and the potholes will still be there next week.)

However, if a blessing is hallowed, it carries the weight of prayer with it. You're invoking divine power or help, and if it's done with sincerity, we can be sure that God hears our prayer. Blessings, certainly those in the hallowed column, need to be taken seriously. They are not glib throwaway lines. To return to Annie Dillard's image of wearing crash helmets to worship, and being lashed to our pews, we need comparable language and reverence for those blessings we so freely bandy about. They're not mere wishes; they're live ammunition that demands great respect.

Conclusion: Let's begin with a question, posed in *The Interpreter's Bible*: "What therefore is blessedness? It is first the recognition of a divine relationship. Abraham's inner strength and happiness never came from worldly things; they came from his sense of a purpose above this world that was controlling."[20]

A hallowed blessing, in the Christian context, is *a prayer for the well-being of another party*, which can be an individual or a group of people. It can also be a prayer praising God. A hallowed blessing in some way

---

[20]*The Interpreter's Bible*, Vol. 1, p. 574.

seeks to advance or recognize God's kingdom. "Blessing," says Andrew Davison, "involves an alignment with the world to come."[21]

By contrast, that dimension is lacking in what we have termed a colloquial or casual blessing, where the blessing is said colloquially and lacks the implicit link to God's grace or goodness. We will touch on this more frivolous use of *bless* or *blessing* now and again. But our default will be to assume that throughout this book, we are talking about the hallowed or real blessings, presumably the kind you wanted to focus on when you picked up this book.

---

[21] Andrew Davison, *Blessing*, p. 189.

3

Blessings from the Beginning

It seems there's a pattern of a specific blessing being identified in Scripture each time a new part of God's plan is introduced. Here are six examples:

- The creation story itself
- The flood
- The call of Abraham
- The call of Mary to bear the Christ child
- The birth of Jesus, and
- Jesus' blessing on His disciples upon His ascension, as He hands over to them the task of building His church.

One of our six examples listed above is discussed separately in **The Abrahamic Covenant**. So we'll look briefly at the other five instances where God clearly links a blessing to each turning of the page in His story.

First, we find in Genesis at the culmination of God's creating all things, with the arrival on the scene of creatures made in His own image, that: "God blessed them and said to them, 'Be fruitful and increase in number; fill the earth and subdue it.'"[22]

---

[22] Genesis 1:28. Note however that God has previously blessed the animals and birds, in verse 22.

Next comes Noah, and the flood, after which we read: "Then God blessed Noah and his sons, saying to them, 'Be fruitful and increase in number and fill the earth.'"[23] He established a covenant with Noah, promising that never again will there be such a flood—the visible sign of that promise being the rainbow.

Then we move to the New Testament, where Mary's annunciation evokes sheer wonder on her part, as we read in Luke's account of her meeting with her cousin Elizabeth. "When Elizabeth heard Mary's greeting, the baby leaped in her womb, and Elizabeth was filled with the Holy Spirit. In a loud voice, she exclaimed: 'Blessed are you among women, and blessed is the child you will bear!'"[24]

Then follows Mary's magnificent prayer of response, in which she says, "From now on all generations will call me blessed, for the Mighty One has done great things for me—holy is His name."[25]

The gospel of Luke, interestingly, is big on blessing. It uses the term twenty times, more than in any other gospel. Another of those uses comes when Joseph and Mary present the Christ-child to the aging Simeon, who had been assured by the Holy Spirit that he would see the Messiah before he died: "The child's father and mother marveled at what was said about him. Then Simeon blessed them...."[26]

Luke helps us once again with the final example we'll cite, regarding Jesus' ascension. "When he had led them out to the vicinity of Bethany, he lifted up his hands and blessed them. While he was blessing them, he left them and was taken up into heaven. Then they worshiped him and returned to Jerusalem with great joy."[27]

Unsurprisingly, those are Luke's last references to *blessing*. Elsewhere, though, we'll find more examples in Scripture of blessing associated with new beginnings. One is God's blessing of Jacob following their all-night wrestling match. That event leaves Jacob with a new name, signifying the next step in the history of God's chosen people, their identity as "Israel"—most likely meaning "struggles with

---

[23] Genesis 9:1.
[24] Luke 1:41-42.
[25] Luke 1:48-49.
[26] Luke 2:33-34.
[27] Luke 24:50-52.

God." Similarly, in the book of Revelation, pointing us as it does to an entirely new kind of beginning, *blessed* occurs eight times in the *New International Version*.

So what does this barrage of Bible episodes signify for us today? In each instance, we're looking at God's outworking of His message for humankind. And it's a message of good news, as we see in the roots of the word *gospel*, derived from Old English *godspell*, a combination of *good* and *spell* (*talk*, *tale*, *story*, *news*). It is as if each chapter of this good-news story begins with blessing, an act of God once again setting in motion good things and wellbeing for His people. This "good news" begins in Genesis 1 and goes all the way through to Revelation. God is continuously seeking to bring us into a state of blessedness, from the beginning, in the creation story, to the culmination of all history, at the end of time. And we can be sure that the blessings won't end even then.

PART 2

More on the Nature

of Blessings

4

Proposing a Toast

It's your son's wedding and the best man stands to propose a toast. Following a handful of mandatory jokes, and an embarrassing anecdote about your son when he was in ninth grade, the best man says, "So, please stand and join me in a toast to the bride and groom: may they have many years together in their journey of love. To Tanya and Bill." The assembled guests murmur, "To Tanya and Bill," and the festivities continue.

It's not too much of a stretch to imagine God proposing a toast to each one of us today: "May you know my grace in abundance once again this day; may you walk in ways that please and honor me; and may you share my love with all whose lives you touch." And the Triune God says, "Let us toast Abby, Brian, Charlotte, Desmond, Evelyn…"

A toast at a formal event like a wedding or a retirement party publicly proclaims the hope that good things will befall the person or people being honored. Whether or not the event has religious overtones, the call is in effect for a blessing. The person proposing the toast is offering hope. But that is all: He or she has no power to bring it about. By contrast, when the God of the universe who each day "proposes a toast" to our wellbeing, He is both utterly committed to blessing us in innumerable ways—and has the power to make those blessings a reality.

5

Blessing in the Old Testament and the New

Blessing in the Old Testament typically comes in one of two contexts. One is where the children of Israel use *bless* in praise or worship of God. We find that in the expression "Blessed be Yahweh" or "Bless the Lord," as in Psalm 103:

Bless the Lord, O my soul: and all that is within me, bless his holy name.
Bless the Lord, O my soul, and forget not all his benefits....[28]

This type of blessing flows from Israel's covenant relationship with the Lord, and the Israelites' gratitude for all God has done for them. Then, in addition to the God-directed blessings, there are those that God in turn bestows on the Israelites. These reflect a desire or aspiration for the God-blessed life and include concepts like material prosperity, a large family, good crops and large herds, long life, and good health. See for example Deuteronomy 28:4: "The fruit of your womb will be blessed, and the crops of your land and the young of your livestock—the calves of your herds and the lambs of your flocks." Then, four verses later we read, "The Lord will send a blessing on your barns and on everything you put your hand to. The Lord your God will bless you in the land he is giving you."

Also included are safety and freedom from one's enemies, assurances scattered throughout the Psalms that are too numerous to

---

[28] Psalm 103:1-2 (*King James Version*).

cite here. Together, these blessings reflect at least in part a state of **Shalom**, the flourishing life that God wills for His people. The Hebrew word *ashere* or *asre* is translated in the *New International Version*, and many others, as "Blessed is the one…" This phrase appears in the *NIV* eleven times in the Psalms and Proverbs. William Barclay says the word means "O the bliss of…"—a notion explored more fully in the entry on **The Beatitudes**. Like the Greek term used in the Beatitudes, D. E. Garland says *as he re*conveys a sense of congratulations because the recipients of the blessing are in "the enviable position of having divine approval… They are judged to be fortunate because it is assumed that God rewards trust in him with worldly well-being."[29] Eugene Peterson tries to capture the sense of this in Psalm 31 in *The Message*: "Count yourself lucky, how happy you must be…."

The other important Hebrew word we should note is *barak*, or more accurately *brk*, as Hebrew doesn't include the vowels. It conveys a range of meanings, including "bestow goodness or favor or to greet, congratulate, thank, make peace, worship, or praise."[30]

Most references to God's blessing in the Old Testament speak to the nuts and bolts of daily living: the realities of an agrarian people who made their living from the soil and from the flocks, while always under threat of military attack from hostile neighbors. It was God alone, through His covenant relationship with His people, that sustained them and enabled them to flourish—if they kept their side of the covenant. As one writer put it, "[B]lessing in the Old Testament … involves always an awareness or recognition of the promise of Yahweh to uphold his creation and his covenant."[31]

In the New Testament, by contrast, the focus shifts from material to spiritual blessings. "[W]e may say of the New Testament as a whole that it basically modifies, but does not abrogate, the Old Testament view of blessing as Yahweh's constant intervention in

---

[29]D. E. Garland, in *Dictionary of Jesus and the Gospels*, p. 78.
[30] F. Rachel Magdalene, in *Eerdmans' Dictionary of the Bible*, p. 192.
[31]*The Encyclopedia of Christianity*, Vol 1, p. 277.

history through what He has done in Christ. Blessing is now oriented to the saving work of Christ...."[32]

Preeminent are Jesus' Beatitudes, where He identifies the blessings that will accrue to His disciples. In addition, we get scattered throughout Paul's letters various blessings in the form of doxologies and benedictions. The blessing of the new covenant in Jesus is good news for the circumcised and the uncircumcised, as Paul writes in Romans.[33]

Three other references to New Testament blessings and their spiritual rather than material emphasis are:

- In Peter's sermon following the healing of the lame beggar: "When God raised up His servant, he sent him first to you to bless you by turning each of you from your wicked ways."[34]

- In Paul's letter to the Galatians: "Scripture foresaw that God would justify the Gentiles by faith, and announced the gospel in advance to Abraham: 'All nations will be blessed through you.' So those who rely on faith are blessed along with Abraham, the man of faith."[35] And

- In Paul's greeting to the Ephesians: "Praise be to the God and Father of our Lord Jesus Christ, who has blessed us in the heavenly realms with every spiritual blessing in Christ."[36]

Similarly, we get references to the blessing of Jesus overcoming death through His resurrection.[37] In brief, the emphasis in the New Testament is that "the definitive blessing has been bestowed upon mankind in Jesus Christ."[38]

No longer should the focus of God's people be what we eat or drink or wear. As Jesus said in the Sermon on the Mount, God will

---

[32]*The Encyclopedia of Christianity*, Vol 1, p. 278.
[33] Romans 4:11.
[34] Acts 3:26.
[35] Galatians 3:8-9.
[36] Ephesians 1:3.
[37] See Romans 5-8.
[38]*The Interpreter's Dictionary of the Bible*, Vol. 1, p. 447.

take care of these things for us. Our role, in the new order He ushered in, is "… seek first his kingdom and his righteousness, and all these things will be given to you as well."[39] As Jesus' disciples, we should be free of the concerns that understandably dominated God's people in the Old Testament. No longer should we be worried about our equivalent of crops and lands and herds, long lives, large families, and protection from hostile Philistines. Our overriding priority is to seek first God's kingdom and implement it and His righteousness.

---

[39] Matthew 6:33.

6

Who Gets to Bless? And Who Gets Blessed?

There's at least one parallel between blessing and the importance of touch in Western culture. Think of the doctor tending to a patient in the hospital. She finishes a conversation with a caring pat on the patient's shoulder. Or the coach sending a player onto the basketball court, with a pat on the back. Or a caring teacher, doing the same thing to encourage a third-grader who's making progress on a math problem. In each case, it's the person of higher status or of greater power who initiates the touch. Young children haven't yet learned this unspoken rule and will with endearing spontaneity touch whomever they like. But third-graders have learned not to go and pat the teacher on her back.

So too with the blessing of people. Normally, the blessing flows from a person with higher authority to one or more people of lower authority. Think of the pastor or priest giving a blessing at the end of worship.[40] The **Introduction** gave the example of the simple prayers my wife and I prayed over our young children.

Then there are the blessings that God bestows on us mortals, which reflects an infinite gap between the status of the one who blesses and those who receive. It's impossible to imagine a wider gap than the

---

[40] Andrew Davison, in his book titled *Blessing,* provides a thorough overview of the role of blessing in liturgical traditions of the Anglican, Roman Catholic and Orthodox churches.

one between the divine and the human. It's worth noting that God blesses individuals (think of Abraham, Isaac, and Jacob, as well as a man after His own heart, King David) and groups: especially His chosen people, the children of Israel, as well as the worldwide church.

In these examples, we see that the one who blesses is either God or people who have an inherent status that qualifies them to bless, such as a pastor or priest, or a mom or dad saying a good night prayer.

When we look to a source of blessing by people, we expect him or her to have several qualities. One is that this person is genuinely concerned for our wellbeing and that the blessing is truly for our good. It is also necessary that the source has the authority to do the blessing. With God, the authority is inherent in who He is. But with people, the authority is either inherent or assigned. Like a sheriff's deputy or an ambassador to another country, a pastor or priest is accorded a certain authority. They can act only because of the authority they've been given.

To return to the parallel regarding touch, on occasion a person of lower status will go against the norm of who touches whom and reach out to the person of higher status. So a patient may grab a doctor's hand or arm to express gratitude. Or think of the woman we read about in Mark's gospel who had the hemorrhage and reached out to touch the robe of Jesus, someone of far greater status.[41] Even though the touching is by someone of lower status, there's no doubt who is the dominant figure in that interaction.

In each of these settings, the dominant person is the one able to give the blessing—that is, if we're talking about blessings being equivalent to "good things." There's an exception. It has to do with that other meaning of blessing when we talk about people praising or thanking God. In this case, it's ordinary worshippers or their leader

---

[41] Mark 5:26-34.

reaching out to God in worship. Here's an instance where David, on behalf of his people, praises and thanks the Lord:

> *Wherefore David blessed the Lord before all the congregation: and David said, Blessed be thou, Lord God of Israel our father, for ever and ever. ... And David said to all the congregation, Now bless the Lord your God. And all the congregation blessed the Lord God of their fathers, and bowed down their heads, and worshipped the Lord, and the king.*[42]

Is there such a thing as peer-to-peer blessing, that sidesteps the status difference? Yes. Assuming it's done sincerely, any individual can offer a blessing on someone of equivalent status. Consider two friends concluding a conversation and one of them says, "That new job sounds exciting. God bless you as you take on this new challenge." But even then, the person offering this blessing is taking the initiative, and taking on a dominant posture.

So why does all this matter? It doesn't, really, other than to remind us to be aware of our role in God's scheme of things. It may be that we are given a sacred charge over others, either formally or informally. Perhaps it's as a mom or dad, or a school teacher. Or a mid-level manager with authority over the marketing department. We are all potential "blessers" of others. Or maybe we have a subordinate role. If so, let us then seek out the blessings we may be able to derive from others: our pastor or priest, a godly boss, or our men's group Bible study.

The reality is that we fill a mix of roles: that we are both agents *of* blessing and agents *for* blessing. Knowing which role we're filling at any given time in any given context should make us more blessing-conscious—or to use a tennis metaphor, whether we are in serving or receiving mode, which might give a whole new meaning to the old joke about Moses serving in the courts of Pharaoh, at 5-3 in the second set.

---

[42] 1 Chronicles 29:10, 20 (*King James Version*).

7

Blessings and Curses

Why, you may reasonably ask, is there an entry in a book on blessings that touches on the opposite concept, that of curses? The answer is that the book would be incomplete without considering this less familiar and more unpleasant notion. Christians tend to overlook the Old Testament. Or, to the extent we pay attention to it, we may be inclined to brush off or disregard aspects that we find distasteful, primitive or (and let's be honest here) even unworthy of the love that Jesus manifests in the New Testament. Things like stoning adulterers, not eating shellfish, or urging the killing of men, women and children in a captured town. If we're inclined to downplay these unpleasantries, we're only too willing to add curses to the list of things-not-to-be-discussed.

But we can't escape them. Indeed, one scholar writes, "Curse and blessing are among the basic organizing concepts of the book of Genesis...The Priestly author of Genesis 1 places the divine blessing on humankind at the beginning of his work; but the Yahwist chapters that follow are a narrative dominated by God's curse, from the man and the woman to Cain to the flood...."[43] It's a topic so central to understanding blessings that Andrew Davison accords it a full chapter in his study.[44]

---

[43] *Harper's Bible Dictionary*, p. 199.
[44] Andrew Davison, *Blessing*, ch. 5.

An especially important treatment of blessings and curses comes in Deuteronomy, where the Lord lays out a covenantal agreement with His people. Following the pattern of treaties made between rulers and their subjects, or treaties between rulers, God says this is what I will do for you and in return, you are required to do this for me. Beginning in chapter 27, we read that Moses commands the people:

When you have crossed the Jordan, these tribes shall stand on Mount Gerizim to bless the people: Simeon, Levi, Judah, Issachar, Joseph and Benjamin. And these tribes shall stand on Mount Ebal to pronounce curses: Reuben, Gad, Asher, Zebulun, Dan and Naphtali.[45]

Then follows a list of the curses that will ensue if the Israelites commit certain offenses, like moving a boundary stone, leading the blind astray, or breaking any of several sexual taboos.

The next chapter begins with the most powerful of little words, *if.* For it is here that God spells out the conditions that His people must follow if they are to know His blessings:

If you fully obey the Lord your God and carefully follow all his commands I give you today, the Lord your God will set you high above all the nations on earth. All these blessings will come on you and accompany you if you obey the Lord your God.[46]

The next eleven verses detail the specific blessings God has in mind. They range from big-picture prosperity for the land and families to the blessing of "your basket and your kneading trough."[47] Then follows another *if* and another list of curses that will ensue if the Israelites do not obey God's commands. They do not make for cheerful reading.

Numerous other references to curses and cursing occur in the Old Testament, which we won't explore here. That's because these several chapters in Deuteronomy give us an excellent and sufficient understanding of God's main message to us: "If you choose me and my commands, you will be blessed; if you reject me and my

---

[45] Deuteronomy 27:12-13.
[46] Deuteronomy 28:1-2.
[47] Deuteronomy 28:5.

commands, you will bring curses upon yourself." It all hinges on that little word, *if*, as the Lord presents the Israelites the most fateful choice they could make: "I have set before you life and death, blessings and curses. Now choose life, so that you and your children may live...."[48]

---

[48] Deuteronomy 30:19.

8

Blessings are for People, not Things

In July 2014, Queen Elizabeth had yet another of those routine royal duties. This one, though, had a decidedly non-routine dimension, as she participated in the launch of a Royal Navy aircraft carrier. She culminated her remarks with a traditional formula adapted for the occasion: "I name this ship Queen Elizabeth. May God bless her and all who sail in her."

Like countless vessels before, this state-of-the-art addition to the Royal Navy sailed forth under a blessing—from no other than the monarch after whom it was named.

So why do we have this tradition of blessing things? And which things merit a blessing? The act of blessing a ship offers us a brief case study to answer those two questions. It seems that we call down God's blessing on those things, like ships, that have one or both of these qualities: the blessing is for something substantive, that is expected to have long use, and it is something that may be associated with danger. It's not without reason that hymns and prayers have been written for those at sea. A hymn from the 1800s, by William Whiting, has the lines:

O hear us when we cry to Thee,
For those in peril on the sea.

The hymn, "Eternal Father Strong to Save," was popularized by the Royal Navy and the United States Navy, and is in frequent use by navy chaplains. It is no coincidence that the poet and clergyman George Herbert wrote, "He that will learn to pray, let him go to sea."

Given the hazards facing seafarers, especially in days gone by, it's understandable why they would welcome whatever protection a blessing might afford their vessel.

But there's a crucial distinction to be made between the vessel itself, and the people for whose safety we are concerned. We bless things because of the *people* associated with them, not for a *thing's* own sake. Our action asks God to protect the ship only because it will carry vulnerable people. The ship itself doesn't become a beneficiary of prayer.

We also bless things like our houses, or more accurately, our homes. Let's look at two approaches. The first is a simple Kenyan prayer:

> *May the person who is going to live in this house have many children, may he be rich; may he be honest to people and good to the poor; may he not suffer from disease or any other kind of trouble; may he be safe all these years.*

Although in its brevity it doesn't say much about the house, it seeks a shalomic future for its occupant. By contrast, the *New Zealand Prayer Book's* liturgy for the blessing of a home runs to twelve pages. The introduction says, "The blessing of a home encourages Christians to dedicate their life at home to God and to others." The liturgy then provides for those participating to move around the outside, as the priest cites Scripture and prays, followed by additional Scripture readings and prayer as the group moves through the various rooms in the new home.[49]

---

[49] The Catholic *Book of Blessings* provides the Church's priests with an astonishing array of blessings in its 896 pages, to be used in the widest imaginable range of settings.

Surely these blessings of ships and our homes please God, as we invoke His care. Most likely, He would be pleased too if we asked God's blessing on a new car, for the safety of all who will ride in it.

There's a danger, though, of trivializing the holiness associated with God's blessing. Are we to seek His blessing on our new deep fryer? "That reminds me: did I ask You, Lord, to bless my new potato peeler—and if I didn't, can I still do so? And what about my new yellow highlighter...?"

Is there some rule of thumb we can follow to avoid such silliness? Maybe the way to go is to recognize that every new item (a tool, a car, or even that yellow highlighter) is a part of God's overall goodness in our lives. Feeling obliged to ask God's blessing on every little thing that may come our way could lead to an obsession, and guilt over the items we may have missed. Instead, God is probably grateful for our overall gratitude.

The point is that we bless God out of thanks or praise, or we bless our fellow humans. We need to beware that we don't attribute blessedness to objects in the sense that they now have some magical or special power. When we bless a house, a ship, a meal, a cross, or a rosary, we are seeking God's grace and goodwill on the people who will use those items. There's nothing magical or superstitious about blessings. Nor should we attribute such powers to mere things, whether they've been blessed or not.

9

Blessings Made Tangible

G od made us sensory people. Yes, we can think about the nature of blessings. We can debate the theology behind the blessing of confession and forgiveness. And we can caution our fellow Christians who are in danger of slipping into "prosperity gospel" thinking as they misconstrue the meaning of the material blessings God has given them.

But we're still sensory people, people who touch, smell, hear, taste and see. So it's not surprising to see that many blessings recorded in Scripture are accompanied by tangible physical gestures. Think for example of Jacob's blessing of his grandchildren, Manasseh and Ephraim, recounted in Genesis 48. Joseph notices his father placing his right hand for the first blessing on the younger brother, Ephraim, and tries to correct him. Jacob insists on breaking with protocol and gives priority to Ephraim.

We could profitably explore the significance of Jacob's action, and how it relates to how he and his mother, Rebekah, deceived Isaac and cheated Esau out of his blessing—again done by laying on of hands. Instead, our interest here is solely on how the blessings were given: a highly tactile gesture, using the hands.

We see similar examples in the New Testament, as in Acts where seven men are chosen to help organize the food relief program.[50] The apostles then lay hands on them, thus blessing them and equipping

---

[50] Acts 6:6.

49

them for their ministry. And when Jesus is asked to bless the children, He does so by placing His hands on them.

Then, in another setting altogether, His ascension, Jesus again uses His hands in blessing: "When he had led them out to the vicinity of Bethany, he lifted up his hands and blessed them."[51] In doing so, Jesus was following a practice that had a long history with the children of Israel. To cite one example, from Leviticus: "Then Aaron lifted his hands toward the people and blessed them. And having sacrificed the sin offering, the burnt offering and the fellowship offering, he stepped down."[52]

That practice of uplifting hands in blessing carries on even today; at the end of Christian worship services around the world as a pastor or priest gives the benediction. Or it may be the hand gesture giving the sign of the cross that accompanies a pastoral blessing.

While hands are such powerful instruments associated with giving a blessing, they are not the only ones. Two others are the use of holy water and oil used in anointing people, such as Samuel's singling out Saul and then David as God's chosen ones.

Then consider baptism, whether it's that of Jesus Himself, the Ethiopian eunuch, or the 3,000 who were baptized on Pentecost. Water, in both its domestic and symbolic uses, is central to our lives— and as it's used in baptism, to our spiritual lives in particular.

Finally, let's look at the Lord's supper or the Eucharist. There's nothing more down to earth than food and drink. So it is not surprising that Jesus chose bread and wine as the instruments by which we are to remember Him. He didn't just say, "do this in remembrance of me."[53] He gave us something tangible by which to do so. We are made of stuff; we are physical beings. God's repertoire of blessings is often associated with stuff.

The ultimate example of "blessings-as-stuff" is the incarnation, which shows how God related to us in the flesh. By becoming part of

---

[51] Luke 24:50.
[52] Leviticus 9:22.
[53] Luke 22:19.

the same dust of which we are made, Jesus became one whom we could perceive through our senses. He became tangible.

In one scriptural example after another, then, culminating in the incarnation itself, we see blessings that have physical components that we can touch, taste, see, smell and hear. It is as the psalmist said, we are invited to "Taste and see that the Lord is good."[54]

---

[54] Psalm 34:8.

10

Stealth Blessings

But when you pray, go into your room, close the door and pray to your Father, who is unseen. Then your Father, who sees what is done in secret, will reward you.

—Matthew 6:6

Most of us aren't in formal roles that authorize us to give a blessing, as discussed in the entry, **Who Gets to Bless? And Who Gets Blessed?** But we should recognize that all of us are empowered to pray for others in need. Therefore, if we see a blessing as a prayer for someone else's wellbeing, there's every reason for us to pray for others. Yet we ordinary Christians, not endowed with any formal authority, still have a great capacity to bless others that we may not be aware of. As James says, "The prayer of a righteous person is powerful and effective."[55]

So, pray for old Mrs. Evert in the women's group at church, who had a stroke last week; for Gary at work, who has that big presentation later today; and for that obviously distressed young woman you noticed in the car next to yours as you waited at the light this morning. Ask God to bring goodness into their lives. Whether they're people you know or strangers, take advantage of your access to a God who hears all prayers and cares for all people as you pray your blessing on them.

---

[55] James 5:16.

Of course, we should be praying for others as we live out our faith; as the *Catechism of the Catholic Church* states, "[E]very baptized person is called to be a 'blessing,' and to bless."[56] Think of those countless Christian teachers in US public schools who need to carefully straddle the wall separating church and state. No wall can stop them from praying silently and secretly for the children in their care, especially the needy or troubled ones. Nor can anyone in the office stop you from praying for the woman in accounts receivable who's struggling with her marriage. Indeed, one could ask if you're not engaging in at least some stealthy, blessing-seeking prayer for others, why aren't you?

---

[56] Quoted in Andrew Davison, *Blessing*, p. 167.

11

The Beatitudes

The Yiddish word *chutzpah* means brazen cheek or sheer audacity. One classic, and humorous, example is that of a man who murders his parents and then casts himself at the mercy of the court because he's an orphan. Another is a cartoon of a fellow in a bookstore who says to the clerk, "I want a book on chutzpah and I want you to pay for it."

So keep chutzpah in mind as you read this section. It certainly takes some cheek to think there's anything original to say about the Beatitudes. Hundreds (maybe thousands?) of books have been written about Jesus' famous sermon on the mount (in Matthew's gospel) or on the plain (as it is recorded in Luke). The chutzpah gets notched up another level when we consider the difficulty of translating the word *blessed* in Jesus' sermon. "[T]ranslators of these beatitudes despair of finding equivalents in English (should 'blessed' be replaced by 'happy' or 'fortunate'?). The problem remains: How to do justice to the conjunction of divine and human activity in a language that limits itself to human relationships."[57] But because this is Jesus' statement par excellence on the state of blessedness, there's no escaping its importance in any exploration of our topic. We will limit ourselves to six observations about Jesus' assertions of blessedness. For the sake of brevity, we'll concentrate only on Matthew's treatment. But first, let's read them again, in the *New International Version*, bearing in mind that

---

[57] Paul S. Minear, in *The Oxford Essential Guide to Ideas and Issues of the Bible*, p. 74.

most scholars count these as eight beatitudes as they regard the last two verses as one blessing.

> *Blessed are the poor in spirit,*
> *for theirs is the kingdom of heaven.*
> *Blessed are those who mourn,*
> *for they will be comforted.*
> *Blessed are the meek,*
> *for they will inherit the earth.*
> *Blessed are those who hunger and thirst for righteousness,*
> *for they will be filled.*
> *Blessed are the merciful,*
> *for they will be shown mercy.*
> *Blessed are the pure in heart,*
> *for they will see God.*
> *Blessed are the peacemakers,*
> *for they will be called children of God.*
> *Blessed are those who are persecuted because of righteousness,*
> *for theirs is the kingdom of heaven.*
> *Blessed are you when people insult you, persecute you and falsely say all kinds of evil against you because of me.*
> *Rejoice and be glad, because great is your reward in heaven, for in the same way they persecuted the prophets who were before you.*[58]

1. The first point is to note what many commentators emphasize: The Beatitudes are spoken to *Jesus' disciples*. They are not intended for the curious, even the well-intentioned. Only those who have thrown in their lot with Jesus can hope, with the Holy Spirit's help, to rise to the extraordinarily exacting standards of conduct Jesus expects in the Sermon on the Mount (and in Luke's version as well). Part of that sermon includes the blessings Jesus promises His followers. We need to see the Beatitudes in the context of the whole sermon. John Stott writes that for someone to embrace the sermon presupposes an acceptance of the gospel and an experience of conversion. "So the beatitudes set forth the blessings which

---

[58] Matthew 5:3-12.

God bestows (not as a reward for merit but as a gift of grace) upon those in whom he is working such a character."[59]

2. Translators struggle to convey the full extent of what we typically read as *blessed*. The *Amplified Version's* attempt to capture the richness and range of the Greek word *makarios* shows this difficulty. This version gives a virtual thesaurus of concepts in treating "Blessed are the poor in spirit, for theirs is the kingdom of heaven," the first of the Beatitudes in Matthew: *Blessed (happy, to be envied, and spiritually prosperous—with life-joy and satisfaction in God's favor and salvation, regardless of their outward conditions) are the poor in spirit (the humble, who rate themselves insignificant), for theirs is the kingdom of heaven.*[60] We're so accustomed to reading or hearing in English the wording "Blessed are..." that we may fail to grasp the expansive nature of the original Greek.

3. The word *makarios* has an array of connotations, which are easily overlooked in our default translation of *blessed*. The quotation from the *Amplified Bible* above made that clear. But William Barclay again comes to our help by bringing his vast knowledge of the Greek language and culture to our discussion. He says that *makarios* "... describes a bliss which belongs only to the gods. Although the word lost something of its greatness and came to be used in a wider and looser sense, the fact remains that in Greek thought only the gods were truly *hoi makaroi*, the Blessed Ones. In the New Testament itself, God Himself is twice described by this word."[61] He concludes that "The promised bliss [in the Beatitudes] is nothing less than the blessedness of God. Through Jesus Christ, the Christian comes to share in the very life of God."[62]

4. If Christians struggle to grasp the meaning of the Beatitudes, non-Christians make even less sense of Jesus' seemingly paradoxical assertions. For the implication of the Beatitudes is nothing short of revolutionary. As one commentary puts it, "Jesus turns ordinary

---

[59] John Stott, *The Message of the Sermon on the Mount*, p. 37
[60] Matthew 5:3 (*The Amplified Bible*, Classic Edition).
[61] William Barclay, *The Plain Man Look at the Beatitudes*, p. 12. The two passages Barclay goes on to cite are 1 Timothy 1:11 and 6:15.
[62] William Barclay, *The Plain Man Look at the Beatitudes*, p. 13.

human ideas about happiness upside down. Contrary to general opinion, it is not the go-getters, the tough ones, those who bend the rules, who are the real successes. The truly happy ones are those who recognize the spiritual poverty (verse 3) of self-reliance and learn to depend wholly on God."[63] It is that total dependence on God that Jesus expects of His disciples, those whom He was addressing 2,000 years ago as well as us today. This apparent paradox of where true happiness lies is mirrored in the remaining Beatitudes. As Simon Tugwell says, the Beatitudes "seem almost to canonize qualities which are the very antithesis of all achievement and success."[64] How can those who mourn be expected to be happy? Or how can the meek expect to inherit the earth? Well, in God's topsy-turvy world that upends human values, that's precisely what will happen. Tony Campolo told a story about someone sneaking into a large department store and mischievously mixing up the price tags on everything. A large screen TV would be priced at $9.99, for example, or an ordinary bath towel's new price was an absurd $1,800. Campolo's point is that this is what God's economy is like: The things God values may not be what we value, and vice versa. As Isaiah says, "For my thoughts are not your thoughts, neither are your ways my ways," declares the Lord. "As the heavens are higher than the earth, so are my ways higher than your ways and my thoughts than your thoughts."[65]

5. The Beatitudes follow a well-known literary formula from Jesus' time. Known as *macarisms*, from *makarios* mentioned above, these blessings were found in Greek, Egyptian and Hebrew literature. These blessings were used to introduce a brief summary of essential doctrines. In addition, William Barclay, in *The Plain Man Looks at the Beatitudes*, says we need to pay attention to how the Beatitudes are introduced. The *King James Version* has: "And he opened his mouth, and taught them, saying...."[66] This version accurately includes the Greek word for *mouth*, unlike translations

---

[63] *The Lion Handbook to the Bible*, p. 478.
[64] Simon Tugwell, *The Beatitudes: Soundings in Christian Traditions*, p. 1. Italics in original.
[65] Isaiah 55:8-9.
[66] Matthew 5:2 (*King James Version*).

that go for a more idiomatic or equivalent expression in English, like the *NIV's* "he began to teach them." This wording "opened his mouth" is significant, Barclay says, because it is an expression that is "…regularly used to introduce any weighty, grave and important utterance…. By using this phrase of Jesus, Matthew warns us that there is to follow an utterance of the greatest weight and importance…."[67] He's right. As the French bishop Jacques-Bénigne Bossuet said, "If the Sermon on the Mount is the precis of all Christian doctrine, the eight Beatitudes are the precis of the whole Sermon on the Mount."[68]

6. Depending on how they are counted (as eight or nine), the Beatitudes in Matthew's gospel are easily divided into either two or three sections or stanzas. John Stott divides them into two groups of four, saying that the first four blessings describe the Christians' relationship to God; the second four describe our relations and duties to other people. Commentators who divide them into three stanzas say that the first stanza reflects conditions where Jesus' followers stand in need of God's help. These are to overcome their poverty of spirit, to be comforted when mourning, and to avoid being taken advantage of because of their meekness. People in these situations need God's intervention and saving. The second stanza "shows qualities of a way of life created by God's saving presence."[69] These three refer to those who hunger and thirst for righteousness, the merciful, and the pure in heart. The third stanza refers to the peacemakers, those who are persecuted because of righteousness, and those who are insulted and persecuted for Jesus' sake. This last stanza speaks to harmony in the community.[70]

7. Scholars vary in their opinion on when this state of blessedness Jesus promises will occur. Will it be in the present? Are the poor, those who mourn, and so on to attain this state of blessedness in the here and now? Or is this a state to be attained only in the

[67] William Barclay, *The Plain Man Look at the Beatitudes*, pp. 8-9.
[68] Quoted in Simon Tugwell, *The Beatitudes: Soundings in Christian Traditions*, p. 1. Bossuet lived from 1627 to 1704.
[69] Warren Carter, in *Eerdmans' Dictionary of the Bible*, p. 159.
[70] Warren Carter, in *Eerdmans' Dictionary of the Bible*, p. 159.

future? In what we call the parable of the talents (and which the *NIV* calls the parable of the bags of gold), Jesus tells what happens to the servant who doubles the money he was given: "His master replied, 'Well done, good and faithful servant! You have been faithful with a few things; I will put you in charge of many things. Come and share your master's happiness!'"[71] Is this "happiness" to be experienced only at a future time? On the other hand, taking the Beatitudes in context, it seems obvious that Jesus was speaking to His followers about aspects of discipleship in their own situations, in the present. John Stott argues that the Beatitudes apply to both the present and the future.[72] For our purposes, we will assume Stott is correct, and that we twenty-first-century Christians, like all Christians before us, should attend carefully to these paradoxical promises of our Lord. We need to learn more fully how we are blessed in the present and live out the kind of lives Jesus hoped for among those who heard that initial sermon more than two thousand years ago.

How are we to conclude this discussion? Tugwell says:

In our meditations on the Beatitudes it is quite crucial that we keep bringing them back to ourselves, reminding ourselves that "this means me." It is not "they" who are poor, it is I myself. And what is being said is not "those poor, poor people, what can we do about it?" but "you blessed poor people, blessed are you." ... It is when we feel ourselves to be poor, humiliated, desperate and all the rest of it that we qualify for the label "blessed."[73]

When we have emptied ourselves to the point of spiritual poverty, where we have nothing of our own to draw upon, God stands ready to fill that void with a love that makes us blessed indeed.

---

[71] Matthew 25:21.

[72] John Stott, *The Message of the Sermon on the Mount*, p. 34.

[73] Simon Tugwell, *The Beatitudes: Soundings in Christian Traditions*, p. 15.

12

Blessings as Permission

Act 3, Scene 2: Lord Wimberley's living room, furnished in classical Victorian style.

Lord Wimberley is in evening dress, smoking his pipe while reading The Times. *Enter stage left his daughter, Agapantha, known to all as Aggie. She's a tall, slightly built young woman of 19. She is wearing 1920s tennis gear and is holding a wooden racket.*

Aggie (exhilarated): Daddy, Daddy… You'll never guess what happened!

Lord Wimberley: Hmmm…

Aggie (more exhilarated): Bobby has asked me to marry him!

Lord Wimberley (perking up slightly): Hmmm?

Aggie (even more exhilarated): Bobby, Daddy—he's asked me to marry him!

Lord Wimberley (empties his pipe and slowly refills it): Bobby, you say? Old Ransom's son?

Aggie: Yes!

Lord Wimberley (now fully engaged): Hmmm…. The groundskeeper's boy, you mean?

Aggie: Yes, yes? Will you give us your blessing, Daddy?

[Thunder clap and lightning; stage goes dark. Curtain closes.]

W ell, *will* Lord Wimberley give his blessing? We are left to decide for ourselves. Meanwhile, though, we'll explore the nature of blessing as permission or approval. Normally, we think of someone, like Aggie, seeking a blessing or endorsement for a certain step or course of action that is marked by some hesitancy, uncertainty, or even probable opposition. Will Daddy find the prospect of his only daughter marrying the groundskeeper's son an unimaginable match, no matter how much Aggie and Bobby might affirm their love for each other?

Or take another scenario: Your son is studying biology at college and during the Thanksgiving break announces that he's no longer committed to following a pre-med course. He wants to study philosophy/art/history/theatre or whatever instead. Does he have your blessing? he asks.

We don't usually ask people for their blessing unless it's for a choice that is likely to meet with opposition—or at least a lack of enthusiasm. ("Well, my boy, you can study whatever you want, whatever makes you happy. But expect no more tuition dollars from us from now on.")

It's significantly different, though, when it comes to seeking God's approval. Surely, we shouldn't even approach Him for His blessing if we're looking at a course of action we think He might not approve. As G. C. Lichtenberg put it, "Never undertake anything for which you wouldn't have the courage to ask the blessings of heaven."[74] We wouldn't dream of asking God's blessing on a weapons smuggling venture or embezzling from the office ("But it's for the widows and orphans, Lord"). No, these are clearly off-limits. Other, seemingly innocent, opportunities might not present choices so obviously displeasing to God. What about taking that job in Sacramento? Maybe you have serious doubts about the wisdom of accepting what is a highly attractive offer. But there's still something that doesn't sit right with the decision. For you to go ahead and ask God's blessing on something about which you remain doubtful is surely a foolish move.

---

[74] Quoted in *Topical Encyclopedia of Living Quotations*, ed. Sherwood Wirt, p. 19.

Then there's another category. Let's say that the combination of prayer, your understanding of Scripture, and the counsel of wise friends leads you to conclude that it is indeed God's will for you to take that Sacramento job. Even though you're nervous about committing to this move, you are confident that this is indeed God's will for you. Now, working from a position of strength, is the time to move ahead, asking God's blessing on a decision you've made in good faith. You hold fast to the words of J. Oswald Sanders, who said, "Having come to a... prayerful decision after having renounced personal preference and prejudice, there is no reason to review or question your guidance. *Never dig up in unbelief what you have sown in faith.* Begin with the confidence that God will guide, and end with the assurance that he has guided."[75] And blessed.

---

[75] Quoted in Gordon S. Jackson, *A Handbook for Discovering God's Will,* p.172. Italics in original.

13

Blessings in Disguise

Winston Churchill, the prime minister who inspired Britain to victory in World War II, suffered an ignominious defeat in the first post-war election in 1945. After being told that this defeat was somehow a "blessing in disguise," he said: "If this is a blessing, it is certainly very well disguised." Maybe it was, because he was restored at age 77 to his position as PM in 1951.

Then there's the old story told about things not always being what they seem, which we'll adapt to make a point about blessings in disguise.

A Chinese man and his son had a much-valued horse that helped the family on their farm. One day the horse ran away and the other villagers said, "What bad luck!" The farmer, always the optimist, replied, "Maybe it's a blessing in disguise."

After several days, the horse returned, bringing several other horses back to the farm as well. The villagers said, "What good luck!" The farmer replied, "Maybe it's a blessing in disguise."

Then came a tragedy. The farmer's son was trying to tame one of the wild horses when he fell off and broke his arm. The neighbors said, "What bad luck!" Again, the optimistic farmer said, "Maybe it's a blessing in disguise."

A few weeks later, soldiers from the national army marched through town, recruiting all boys for the army. They did not take the farmer's son, because of his broken arm. Once again the other villagers said, "What good luck!" And once again the farmer said, "Maybe it's a blessing in disguise."

The problem this story highlights is that we can never be sure of the bigger picture and of what might come next. What seems like the "bad luck" the farmer and son experienced may in fact be the precursor to something good. And conversely, something that seems a blessing may, in God's greater plans for us, be only temporary and replaced by what others would define as bad luck. Christians believe that in the long run, all will be well. As Italian writer Ugo Betti puts it, "To believe in God is to know that all the rules will be fair and that there will be wonderful surprises."[76]

Given our limited knowledge regarding our present circumstances, where we see only part of the picture, we need to understand blessings conditionally or provisionally. All the good things that we have today could be gone tomorrow. Today's blessing of good health may be shattered tomorrow by an out-of-the-blue diagnosis of terminal cancer. Or our splendid six-bedroom mansion by the lake is consumed by wildfire.

We need to make a further distinction, however. The blessings the Chinese farmer was wisely accepting as provisional, as well as blessings like our health and wealth, are all temporal. While being grateful for the good things God gives us (and we have something to say about that six-bedroom mansion elsewhere), we should never lose sight of their temporal nature. Instead, we should focus on the blessing of our having been adopted into God's family, of being declared God's children.[77]

Similarly, when the equivalent of a runaway horse or a broken arm occurs in our lives, we must affirm that this is not the end of the story. Or as Ray Edman puts it, "Taken separately, the experiences of

---

[76] Quoted in Gordon S. Jackson, *Quotes for the Journey, Wisdom for the Way*, p. 60.
[77] See for example Ephesians 1:5.

life can work harm and not good. Taken together, they make a pattern of blessing and strength the like of which the world does not know."[78]

---

[78] Quoted in *Topical Encyclopedia of Living Quotations*, ed. Sherwood Wirt, p. 19.

14

An Abundance of Blessing

"Bring the whole tithe into the storehouse, that there may be food in my house. Test me in this," says the Lord Almighty, *"and see if I will not throw open the floodgates of heaven and pour out so much blessing that there will not be room enough to store it."*

—*Malachi 3:10*

.... how much more will your Father in heaven give good gifts to those who ask him!

—*Matthew 7:11*

These two verses convey a vivid picture of God's storehouse of blessings, ready to be infused into our lives without any worries about supply chain issues. Several things are worth noting about these two verses, and what they say about God's eagerness to bless.

The first is God's eagerness to give us good things. We learn that He is ready to "throw open the floodgates of heaven," unleashing an outpouring of goodness. Notice the energy and vividness of the wording: *throw open* and *floodgates*. This isn't some "ho-hum/oh well/I-might-as-well" activity God's talking about. To continue with the *floodgate* imagery, it's as if God is bursting to bless us. It's as Augustine said, "God is more anxious to bestow His blessings on us than we are to receive them."[79]

Then there's the volume of blessings. There's so much of the stuff that it almost sounds as if He's struggling to hold back this massive build-up of blessings. In another context, Frederick Pollock wrote, "I forget how many thousand eggs go wrong for one codfish that gets hatched. But … it is idle to censure the creation as wasteful if you believe in a creator who has unlimited stuff to play with."[80] Just as God created a super-abundance of life, as Pollock says, we serve a creator who has unlimited grace and blessing to send our way.

It is no wonder that the prophet Malachi records the Lord as saying we won't be able to store all the goodness God wants to give us.

Finally, we must heed the conditional nature of this pent-up supply of blessings. Malachi records the Lord as saying we need to "bring the whole tithe" into God's storehouse. Not only are we to honor God with our giving, but it needs to be the *whole* shebang. No half-hearted giving here…. That means our money, of course, but also our very lives as we present ourselves as a living sacrifice to God.[81]

The lavish outpouring of blessings is thus dependent on a right relationship with our Lord. But that's not all. As Jesus says toward the end of the Sermon on the Mount, we also need to ask our heavenly father for the good gifts that are ours, quite literally, for the asking. No matter how much we have been blessed, God always stands ready to give us more. Consider David, who had received so much as King of Israel yet chose to pursue an adulterous relationship with Bathsheba and arranged the death of her husband. Then God, speaking through the prophet Nathan, said, "I gave you all Israel and Judah. And if all this had been too little, I would have given you even more."[82]

Yes, even more. It's as if yet another shipment of God's blessings is waiting for us in an Amazon locker—a package so large we might need help carrying it to the car.

---

[79] Quoted in Mitch Finley, *The Saints Speak to You Today*, entry no. 68.
[80] Quoted in Gordon S. Jackson, *Outside Insights: Quotations for Contemporary South Africa*, p. 67.
[81] Romans 12:1.
[82] 2 Samuel 12:8.

15

The Responsibility of Being Blessed

William Barclay tells of Lord Dunsany, who after surviving the horrors of trench warfare in World War I, said: "In some strange way I am still alive. I wonder what God means me to do with a life so specially spared?"[83] He subsequently used his talents as a gifted and prolific writer and was the author of more than ninety books. A man of keen intellect and a superb chess player, he also invented an alternative form of the game.

But it is his probing question that merits our attention: "What does God mean me to do with a life so specially spared?" In asking that question, Dunsany was echoing Jesus' words in Luke's gospel: "From everyone who has been given much, much will be demanded; and from the one who has been entrusted with much, much more will be asked."[84]

Presumably, you have not experienced anything comparable to trench warfare in World War I, where as an officer, Dunsany saw many of his men killed in action and faced the trauma of being fired upon himself. Yet you may have a story to tell that brought you close to death: a narrow escape in a car accident; a nearly-fatal illness as a child; or a robbery in which you were threatened with a weapon—and were thankful you lost only your phone and camera, not your life.

---

[83] William Barclay, *The Daily Study Bible: The Letter to the Romans*, p. 48.
[84] Luke 12:48.

Even if you haven't had such a life-threatening experience, each of us bears an invisible tattoo on our bodies: *memento mori*, Latin for "Remember you must die." Not to be morbid about it, but each of us is mortal. If you're in your early twenties, the actuarial tables tell us you're almost certain to live many decades yet. Still life comes with no guarantees, as you'll agree if you think of those few peers who met untimely deaths in high school or college.

Perhaps it's best to rephrase Lord Dunsany's question: "I wonder what God means me to do with a life so specially granted in the first place?" You've been given the incomparable gift of life for a reason, a *God-given* reason. And what *does* God mean you to do with that life?

How, indeed, will you do justice to this most profound of blessings: your very existence? How, indeed....

16

Blessings Anticipated

"Singing a *te deum*," a song of praise, "after a famous victory is good but it's a bit obvious. Singing it beforehand is an audacious act of faith," wrote Roger Pooley.[85] Christians are people of faith who can look back on events in our lives and without doubt affirm that God's hand was directing what occurred. We thank God for those blessings we have enjoyed. But if a certain degree of faith is needed to say, "Yes, God did this in my life," rather than fate or coincidence, how much more faith does it take to anticipate blessings that have not yet come our way?

Sort of like the priests leading the children of Israel across the flooded Jordan river. Picture the scene: After forty years of wandering in the desert, they are poised to require a miraculous move by God; there's no way they can cross the river in their own strength. Fortunately, Joshua's leadership is authoritative enough that these always querulous people trust him to lead the way. Well, at least the priests do—and it is on them he calls, as representatives of the people who are carrying the Ark of the Covenant, to take the first steps. Literally. For Joshua conveys the Lord's command: "Tell the priests who carry the ark of the covenant: 'When you reach the edge of the Jordan's waters, go and stand in the river.'"[86] Note how they had to

---

[85] Roger Pooley, *Encounter with God* Scripture Union Bible reading notes. Date unknown.
[86] Joshua 3:8.

enter the water and take their stand as an act of faith *before* the flooding river subsided. That's not unlike God saying, "OK, jump first and then I'll give you your parachute."

Then, "as soon as the priests who carried the ark reached the Jordan and their feet touched the water's edge, the water from upstream stopped flowing"[87]—a blessed and a miraculous crossing, if ever there was one. But almost as remarkable was the anticipation of that blessing by the priests and their leader, Joshua.

Similarly, there's the story in Exodus of Moses and Aaron and their dealings with Pharaoh, as with total confidence they rely on God in predicting which plague will next descend on this obdurate king and his advisors. Here too Moses' relationship with God empowers him to anticipate what for the Egyptians will be just the opposite of blessings. But these plagues will together work to constitute the greatest blessing for the Israelites, freedom from their oppressors.

Later, as God instructs Moses to prepare the Israelites for the Passover meal, there's a curious statement: "Celebrate the Festival of Unleavened Bread, because it was on this very day that I brought your divisions out of Egypt. Celebrate this day as a lasting ordinance for the generations to come."[88] Notice the wording, "I brought your divisions out of Egypt...." This is in the past tense. God is speaking of a future event that they are to remember but refers to it as if it has already happened. In God's eyes, the event is deserving of a *te deum* in advance.

Then there's the well-documented story of a blessing anticipated, this one involving the British evangelist George Müller, a man renowned for his rich prayer life. He was aboard a ship bound for the Canadian city of Quebec, where he had a speaking engagement. But several days out the ship encountered such thick fog that it seemed impossible they would arrive on time.

The George Müller Organization picks up the story on its website, as recorded in the words of the ship's captain. Müller visited the captain on the bridge and told him that he needed to be in Quebec

---

[87] Joshua 3:13.
[88] Exodus 12:17.

that weekend, four days away. He asked the captain to go to the chart room for prayer.

"Mr. Müller," I said, 'do you know how dense the fog is?'"

"'No,' he replied, 'my eye is not on the density of the fog, but on the living God who controls every circumstance of my life.'"

"He got down on his knees and prayed one of the most simple prayers. The burden of his prayer was something like this: 'O Lord, if it is consistent with Thy will, please remove this fog in five minutes. You know the engagement you made for me in Quebec Saturday. I believe it is your will.' "When he finished, I was going to pray, but he put his hand on my shoulder and told me not to pray. 'First, you do not believe he will; and second, I believe he has [answered]. And there is no need whatever for you to pray about it.' I looked at him, and George Müller said. 'Captain. I have known my Lord for forty-seven years, and there has never been a single day that I have failed to gain an audience with the King. Get up, captain, and open the door, and you will find the fog is gone.'"[89] And in yet another dramatic answer to prayer in this man's life, the fog had dissipated. As we look around, then, at examples in Scripture or at the lives of the most saintly among us, we see one instance after another of God's people acting with unwavering anticipation of a future blessing, as they engage in what Roger Pooley described as "an audacious act of faith."

---

[89]https://www.georgemuller.org/devotional/my-eye-is-not-on-the-fog.

17

Seeing is Believing, Blessing is Even Better

Then he said to Thomas, "Put your finger here; see my hands. Reach out your hand and put it into my side. Stop doubting and believe." Thomas said to him, "My Lord and my God!" Then Jesus told him, "Because you have seen me, you have believed; blessed are those who have not seen and yet have believed."

—John 20:27-29

Pity poor Doubting Thomas.[90] For two millennia, this disciple has been branded a doubter, a skeptic. Yes, we have the account in John's gospel of his famous assertion earlier in the chapter, "Unless I see the nail marks in his hands and put my finger where the nails were, and put my hand into his side, I will not believe." Today we might call the man an empiricist. But that expression of doubt is only part one of this momentous chapter in his life.

Part two was his encounter with the risen Christ when Jesus invites him to touch his wounds. Although we do not know if he touched Jesus or not, thanks to the gift of physical sight and his ability to see Jesus in front of him, this skeptical disciple had a radical breakthrough that converted his physical vision into spiritual insight. It was like having successful cataract surgery, a corneal transplant, and

---

[90] This section is excerpted in part from Gordon S. Jackson, *Be Thou My Vision: Light, Sight and the Christian Faith*.

retinal detachment repair all at once. Whatever partial spiritual vision he had until this moment, Thomas now saw his risen Lord for who he was: "My Lord and my God!" His status is forever changed from doubter to the firmest of believers.

We should therefore be calling the man something like "Believing Thomas" or "Thomas the Convinced" or "The Disciple Formerly Known as the Doubter." The habit of the centuries has triumphed, though, and his nickname reflects only his initial skepticism. Jesus commends him for believing, although it was admittedly only because that initial skepticism was overcome. Still, it is impossible to conceive of the joyous blessing that Thomas received that day, with the first-hand assurance that his Lord whom he thought was dead stood here, scars and all, before him. But then, we have Jesus' words that speak directly to all Christians throughout the ages: "Blessed are those who have not seen and yet have believed." Those countless Christians living today, and the even greater numbers who preceded us, have been blessed for their faith in an unseen savior.

That day Thomas saw the results of a miracle, the resurrection. We did not. Philip Yancey says the following about the miracles that Jesus performed: "To those who chose to believe Him, they [miracles] gave even more reason to believe. But for those determined to deny Him, the miracles made little difference. Some things just have to be believed to be seen."[91] So it is with those not present after the resurrection. As Jesus promised, we too are blessed, because by believing we see.

---

[91] Philip Yancey, *Grace Notes*, p. 72.

18

Shalom—A State of Blessedness

Shalom is a Hebrew word that's found a place in our English vocabulary. Broadly speaking, it means *peace*. But by itself, that does the word a great injustice, for the concept is much richer. *Shalom* signifies not only an absence of hostilities or tension (a negative definition), but a condition marked by flourishing: by wholeness, completeness, harmony, prosperity and tranquility. *Shalom* is pointing to a state that is God's ideal for how people should live together. We could summarize the concept as "a state of pure blessedness."

In addition, the word is used in the Bible and even today as a greeting in Hebrew and, in various forms, in other Semitic languages like Arabic.

Because *Shalom* is a Hebrew word, it's understandable that you won't find it in the *King James Version*, *New International Version* and *Revised Standard Version*, to name a few. To get a fuller sense of how the word is treated in Scripture, let's turn to the *Complete Jewish Bible* (or the *CJV*). It uses *Shalom* ninety-six times.

The first is in Leviticus, where God tells the Israelites: "I will give Shalom in the land—you will lie down to sleep unafraid of anyone. I will rid the land of wild animals. The sword will not go through your land..."[92] The *KJV*, *NIV* and *RSV* all translate *Shalom* as peace—understandably, as that is the nearest one-word equivalent we have in English.

---

[92] Leviticus 26:6 (*Complete Jewish Bible*).

Then, when *Shalom* is used as a greeting, for example in the account of the angel approaching a timid Gideon, we have: "But Adonai reassured him, 'Shalom to you, don't be afraid, you won't die!'"[93] Again, the *KJV*, *NIV* and *RSV* use *peace*.

In the New Testament too, the *CJV* uses *Shalom* repeatedly, often as a greeting. Knowing the connotations of the word, it's a greeting rich in meaning; for example, when the angel Gabriel approaches Mary and says, "Shalom, favored lady! Adonai is with you!"[94]

We could keep exploring the *CJV* to discover the wide range of settings in which Scripture uses this power term. But we'll limit ourselves to just one more example, from Paul's letter to the Romans: "So, since we have come to be considered righteous by God because of our trust, let us continue to have Shalom with God through our Lord, Yeshua the Messiah."[95]

In all these examples in the *CJV,* we see richer, more expansive implications of God's blessings and goodness. We have, in keeping with our definition of what it means to be blessed, a goldmine of insights to be derived from the *CJV*. Whether it be a greeting that says in effect, "May you know the flourishing that God seeks for you," or another reference to that ideal state, note that Shalom is always grounded in God's desires for us.

In his speech upon accepting the Nobel Peace Prize in 1984, South African Archbishop Desmond Tutu spoke of his desire for peace and justice in his country. He said, "God's Shalom, peace, involves inevitably righteousness, justice, wholeness, fullness of life, participation in decision-making, goodness, laughter, joy, compassion, sharing and reconciliation." It's difficult to imagine a setting more filled with blessings than this.

---

[93] Judges 6:23 (*Complete Jewish Bible*).
[94] Luke 1:28 (*Complete Jewish Bible*).
[95] Romans 5:1 (*Complete Jewish Bible*).

19

Our Limits to God's Blessings

The poet T. S. Eliot said that "Humankind cannot bear very much reality."[96] We are limited in what we can absorb as individuals. And the same applies to our spiritual lives. Leonard Boase, in *The Prayer of Faith*, writes that there comes a point when we can no longer accept the good things God is giving us. We're saturated like a sponge: "The sponge is full. It is not that there is no more water in the ocean, but the sponge has absorbed what it needs."[97]

The ocean that represents God's grace far exceeds the blessings we are capable of handling; our sponges are full. Or perhaps it's more a matter of our awareness of the blessings we already have. Think for example of a toddler who in his limited way is grateful for breakfast this morning. But he cannot yet grasp the complex chain that brought food into his home, or the economic system that provided his parents with jobs, or the medical system undergirded with phenomenal advances in science that helps to keep him healthy. There's so much goodness out there that he cannot begin to understand.

We adults rightly think we have a fuller grasp of the world around us, and the blessings (and dangers) it contains. But how little even we must know of the full extent of God's goodness to us.

All of us are limited in our intellectual understanding of God's blessings by our ignorance. But Christians concerned with spiritual

---

[96] T. S. Eliot, *Four Quartets: "Burnt Norton,"* part 1.
[97] Leonard Boase, *The Prayer of Faith*, p. 35.

blessings likewise face a ceiling on just how much of God's blessing they can absorb. A Christian with a new or fledgling faith cannot be expected to receive the full range of blessings that a mature Christian would (or *should*) be open to. Take for example the experience of Paul, who wrote to the Corinthians: "I know a man in Christ who fourteen years ago was caught up to the third heaven."[98] As he makes clear later in the chapter, he is referring to himself—and some mystical, indescribably intense spiritual experience, some blessing of the highest order. One commentator says, "It would be futile to speculate on Paul's experience. He would not have us try to penetrate his mind here."[99] But whatever the nature of this spiritual "high," other especially mature Christians have no doubt experienced similar "third heaven" experiences.

These are hyper-spiritual blessings presumably given to only a few of us and are most likely given to those who have the capacity to receive them. A Latin saying captures this idea: *Quidquid recipitur admodum recipientis recipitur* "whatever is received, is received in the manner of the receiver." That is, our ability to receive a blessing is contingent on our "manner," or capacity or openness to God's blessing.

Time for a larger spiritual sponge?

---

[98] 2 Corinthians 12:2.
[99] *The Interpreter's Bible*, vol. 10, p. 405.

20

The Blessing of Unity

How good and pleasant it is
when God's people live together in unity!
It is like precious oil poured on the head,
running down on the beard,
running down on Aaron's beard,
down on the collar of his robe.
It is as if the dew of Hermon
were falling on Mount Zion.
For there the Lord bestows his blessing,
even life forevermore.

—Psalm 133

The emphasis so far in these reflections has been on personal blessings, and how God generously bestows His grace on us individually. Yes, we have touched on **Shalom**, which speaks to corporate living. Yet given the emphasis in the Old Testament on the importance of the family as a unit, as well as the formation of the nation of Israel, we would be remiss if we didn't explore the blessing that arises from unity and people working together as God's people.

The first verse in Psalm 133 in the *King James Version* and many others refers to *brethren* or *brothers*. But other translations, as listed on the Bible Gateway website, include *brothers and sisters*, *families*, *God's people*, and *kindred*. Whatever the best translation, it is unclear exactly who is being referred to in this verse. It's important to bear in mind that this Psalm is one of the Psalms of Ascent, sung by pilgrims en route to Jerusalem to attend one of the three major festivals: Passover, Pentecost, and Tabernacles (or booths). Presumably, these pilgrims had in mind their family groups, but most likely also the unity of all of Israel, a nation grounded in tribal identity that always contained rivalry or, at worst, even enmity. However we translate this first verse, E. M. Blaiklock says, "The key word is 'brethren.' Unity is possible only when men thus regard themselves, sons of a common father, and called to the love that brothers should hold."[100] That common ancestry, as children of the same God, should elicit a unity that transcends the always-present tribal affiliations or other divisions that are inherent in living next to other human beings.

What then are the blessings that flow from the unity spoken of in this psalm? They surely include a sense of common purpose and identity, as God's people, united in their journey to the Temple and united in honoring their God. There would be the spirit of cooperation that we read about in Nehemiah, when the writer explains why they had made excellent progress in restoring the city wall: "…for the people had a mind to work."[101]

In addition to offering the blessing of unity in their community life, God also promises in the final verse "even life forevermore." One commentary on this verse says that "The promise to the nation was one of renewed and continuing life."[102]

Nowadays, we can apply this psalm to the Christian community: "Its theme is the blessing of fellowship and unity, and it can be applied to the human family, the extended family, a community of God's people, or to the unity of Christians."[103]

But notice the wording in verse 1: "How good and pleasant it is *when* God's people live together in unity!" The *when* assumes that we will not always live in unity. Given Israel's experience, that was a fair assumption for the psalmist to include. The history of Israel, whether

---

[100] E. M. Blaiklock, *Commentary on the Psalms: Volume 2*, p. 123.

[101] Nehemiah 4:6 (*King James Version*).

[102] *New Bible Commentary*, p. 504.

[103] *African Bible Commentary*, p. 734.

of its ancestors in the book of Genesis or of later periods, was a history of distinct groups struggling to live in unity. Given our highly individualistic culture in the United States and in many other Western nations, we tend not to find our identity as part of a group—the family, a clan, a tribe, or a nation. We emphasize our personal engagement with faith matters. Compare that with two examples from Scripture, one positive, the other negative. When the Philippian jailor is converted, his whole family is as well.[104] We find a negative instance of an individual's action leading to dreadful consequences for the family unit following the destruction of Ai when Achan's greed leads him to take some of the spoils for himself.[105] He and his family are put to death, an awful outworking of family unity that was normal for the Israelite community, no matter how repugnant it seems to us today.

In contrast to the potential negative consequences of unity when God's will is disobeyed, this psalm speaks of a unity that is declared blessed, like the holy oils upon the priest Aaron or "the dew of the rainless summer that waters the crops."[106]

The blessing referred to in verse 3, therefore, depends on us getting our act together as a prerequisite for God to bless us, for "God's blessing is granted when people live and work together in unity. The full blessing of God is hindered when there is division and disunity in our families or among Christians."[107] Or because of downright disobedience, as Achan would tell us if he were around.

---

[104] Acts 16.
[105] Joshua 7.
[106] *The Catholic Bible: Personal Study Edition*, p. 738.
[107] *African Bible Commentary*, p. 735.

21

The Ultimate Blessing

Paradoxically, the ultimate blessing that Christians will enjoy is one we cannot begin to describe. At least, not yet. We're talking about death, of which John Baillie, a Scottish theologian, says: "Not even the most learned philosopher or theologian knows what it is going to be like. But there is one thing which the simplest Christian knows—he knows it is going to be all right."

Besides it is "all going to be all right," we can extrapolate from Scripture and thoughtful Christians several other things about the state of our blessedness after death. But let's begin with the reality: Death unsparingly pours out hurt upon Christians and non-Christians alike. Yet for the Christian, death ushers in a peculiar paradox. While we too grieve and ache from our loss and separation as much as others, we have a unique view of death—and a unique conviction. That's because Christians of all traditions and denominations, whether Protestant, Catholic or Orthodox, share the profound belief that in death, our loved ones have entered eternal life, spared of further hurt or suffering and never to be separated from the presence of God Himself. And we believe that we too shall follow in their steps. The Christian view of death thus entails comfort, hope, an assurance that God is indeed in control, and the promise of eternal life.[108]

---

[108] This paragraph is adapted from Gordon S. Jackson, *Grace for the Grieving: Words of Comfort in Times of Loss.*

What is the nature of the blessing that we believe awaits us? The Christian's transition from this life to the next is ultimate in two senses. This change will usher in a life marked by a final—that is, an ultimate—blessing. The life we are living now is therefore receiving only a penultimate (or "second from the end") blessing. Our heavenly life will also enjoy an ultimate blessing in the sense of it being the very best, reflecting the unimaginable goodness that will characterize heaven.

Following Jesus' resurrection, we too are assured that we will triumph over death. As the *Book of Common Prayer* puts it, about the end of our mortal bodies and what the future promises, "Earth to earth, ashes to ashes, dust to dust, in sure and certain hope of the resurrection."

While we cannot begin to grasp what heaven will be like, C. S. Lewis may have put his finger on the essence of things. Imagining our response after death and arriving in heaven, he envisages us saying, "Of course! Of course!"[109] Far from it being a state in which we'll indulge in the kinds of enjoyments or blessings we have known in this life, heaven will at the same time be both utterly familiar and radically different. It will not be a place of endless rounds of golf or fine dining. Instead, it will be as if for the second time, we will have emerged from a womb into a life that was previously unimaginable. We can be sure that it will have all the hallmarks of the state of **Shalom** for which we strive in our current existence. As Thomas à Kempis wrote, "Wait for the promise of God, and you will have blessings in abundance in heaven."[110]

For our purposes, perhaps the most important aspect of our transition from this life to the next is that state of blessedness we can anticipate. The Revelation of St. John makes plain the blessed state that awaits us: "I heard a voice out of Heaven, 'Write this: Blessed are those who die in the Master from now on; how blessed to die that way!' 'Yes,' says the Spirit, 'and blessed rest from their hard, hard work.

---

[109] Quoted in Gordon S. Jackson, *Grace for the Grieving: Words of Comfort in Times of Loss.*
[110] Thomas à Kempis, *The Imitation of Christ*, translated by Betty Knott, p. 135.

None of what they've done is wasted; God blesses them for it all in the end."[111]

And amid this blessedness, we may well echo the words of C. S. Lewis: "Of course! Of course!"

---

[111] Revelation 14:13 (*The Message*).

PART 3

Examples and Case Studies

22

The Abrahamic Blessing

The Lord had said to Abram, "Go from your country, your people and your
father's household to the land I will show you.
I will make you into a great nation,
and I will bless you;
I will make your name great,
and you will be a blessing.
I will bless those who bless you,
and whoever curses you I will curse;
and all peoples on earth
will be blessed through you."

—*Genesis 12:1-3*

It is impossible to overstate the importance of these three verses.
They constitute the foundation of the three great Abrahamic
faiths: Judaism, Christianity and Islam. The words *bless* or *blessing*
occur five times in this short passage. The idea of blessing abounds.

While an entire book could be written on the ramifications of
these verses, we'll limit ourselves to four observations here.

God Initiates the Blessing: In the previous chapter, we learn that
Abram (as he then was) moved from his ancestral home of Ur of the
Chaldees to Harran. Genesis 11 doesn't indicate why Abram's father,
Terah, initiated this move. But Abram's journey is not destined to stop
at Harran. After Terah's death, we get for the first time God's direct

interaction with the couple He has chosen to shape history and to work out His divine plan for humankind. That entails moving from Abram's homeland, as verse 1 indicates. It is unclear if God had previously told Abram to leave his home. On the one hand, we have the wording: "The Lord *had* said to Abram…" (emphasis added), as the *New International Version* and many other translations have it. Or maybe this instruction came later; many other translations simply have "The Lord said to Abram…." For our purposes, it doesn't matter. What is important is God's intrusion in Abram's life with the instruction to keep moving from his hometown toward unknown territory: "…a land I will show you." Then comes the promise that God will make of this man a great nation, and the accompanying promise, "I will bless you."

What is noteworthy is that Abram is minding his own business, no doubt adjusting to the new circumstances he faces having accompanied his father as far as Harran. Is this the final stop? What comes next? And how will he know? And what about a family? In a culture where having children was of paramount importance, he must have been increasingly concerned that Sarai had not yet been able to have a child.

Now, into all his questioning comes "The Divine Intruder,"[112] with God taking the initiative in (1) telling Abram what to do, and (2) assuring him of a blessing—and not just any blessing, but that of Yahweh Himself, the one true God. This combination of command/blessing leads to a second point.

<u>Abram/Abraham will himself be a blessing</u>: Next is a repetition of the promise, that Abram's name will become great, not of his own doing but because God will make that happen. Then comes another promise, as he tells Abram, "You will be a blessing." We should emphasize the *you*, as we see a shift from God doing the blessing, to that of His servant being the one who will cause blessing. The text doesn't specify who Abram will bless but we can infer that it will initially be his family, then his descendants who go on to comprise the twelve tribes of Israel, and finally the worldwide Christian church that

---

[112] The title of a book by James Edwards. *The Divine Intruder: When God Breaks Into Your Life*.

(along with Jews and Muslims) all trace their spiritual heritage to the man from Ur of the Chaldees. This extraordinary level of blessing arises from the simple fact that this man trusted God. That's why he is celebrated as a man whose life exemplified faith. As the writer to the Hebrews put it, "By faith, Abraham when called to go to a place he would later receive as his inheritance, obeyed and went, even though he did not know where he was going."[113] It's clear from this point on that God, having chosen Abram to be the founder of the nation of Israel, will be watching over him, protecting him and his descendants. God will ensure that notwithstanding ups and downs that include times of slavery in Egypt and exile in Babylon, Abram's descendants will be a blessed people. And woe to those who would take on these chosen people, as the Egyptians and others could tell you.

The Global Impact: Verse three comes with another promise, that "all peoples on earth will be blessed through you." Abram, as he still was before becoming Abraham in Genesis chapter 17, can have no idea of the extent to which God will fulfill His basic promise of making him "a great nation." This is especially so as late as chapter 17, when he is ninety-nine years old and still childless, when God ironically changes his name to Abraham, which probably means "father of many."

If Abraham and Sarah (who is also renamed in chapter 17) are struggling with the seeming failure of God's promise that they will be the father and mother of many, how much further beyond their grasp is the reality that the entire world—"all peoples on earth"—would one day be blessed because of their readiness to participate in this God-initiated covenant. All Christians around the world owe the blessing of their spiritual heritage to this man, who acted in faith when God called him.

What's in it for us? How then are we to apply this blessing-rich passage to our lives? Just as God seemingly out of nowhere spoke to this man perhaps 3,000 years ago, so too does God speak to us today. The first implication of this reading is for us too to respond to God's calling in our lives, if we haven't already. Moreover, we are to recognize that as with Abraham, we too are on a faith journey through life,

---

[113] Hebrews 11:8.

knowing that God could lead us to unexpected places or to undertake unexpected tasks. Like Abraham, we must be ready to "obey and go, even though we do not know where we are going."

Then, perhaps more surprisingly, we are humbled to learn that God will use us—yes, even us—to bless others with whom we come into contact.

Nor should we forget the lesson of patience that Abraham and Sarah needed to learn, together with the problems that can arise if we try to force God's hand. As Eugene Peterson put it, "The greatest disaster of Abraham's life was that he used Hagar to get what he thought God wanted for him; the great achievement of his life was what God did for him apart from any program or plans that he put into action."[114]

Finally, as members of God's worldwide church, we are both blessed to share in a truly global family of believers, made up of a huge range of cultures, languages and ways of expressing our common faith in worship and in daily life. Indeed, even Abraham, legendary for his faith, would be amazed at what God has wrought because he believed and staked everything on the one true God.

---

[114] Eugene Peterson, *Traveling Light*, p. 131.

23

A Blessing Stolen

Blessings demarcate two pivotal moments in Jacob's life. The first occurs when he is a young man in a dysfunctional family, where his mother talks him into deceiving his twin brother out of the blessing that is Esau's due. It's a tragic story of a mother's prejudice against one son and in favor of another, of a human drama with fraught consequences.

Then there's the equally familiar story of Jacob, now a prosperous man with a family and considerable wealth, en route to meet his long-estranged brother. But first, he has a strange, divine wrestling match, which culminates in a **Blessing Demanded**—obtained through a grueling physical showdown with either God or an angel.

Let's begin with the well-known story of Jacob tricking his brother Esau. Here's the account of Esau's response to having been scammed out of his right as the first-born son.

> *"My father, please sit up and eat some of my game, so that you may give me your blessing."*
> *His father Isaac asked him, "Who are you?"*
> *"I am your son," he answered, "your firstborn, Esau."*
> *Isaac trembled violently and said, "Who was it, then, that hunted game and brought it to me? I ate it just before you came and I blessed him—and indeed he will be blessed!"*
> *When Esau heard his father's words, he burst out with a loud and bitter cry and said to his father, "Bless me—me too, my father!"*

But he said, "Your brother came deceitfully and took your blessing."[115]

Not only did Jacob deceive his father through carefully planned treachery, but he also commits blasphemy by lying and saying the Lord helped him to find the hunted game so quickly.[116] Yet, beside the drama, the betrayal, the blasphemy, and the dynamics of a dysfunctional family, the story is all about blessing: who gets to give it, to whom, why and how, and to what end. One other thing: why can it not be reversed? To those of us in the West who are aware of carefully worked out laws about contracts, Jacob obtained the blessing by crafty yet utterly fraudulent means. He and his conniving mother would not have been treated kindly in a twenty-first-century US court. Yet it's clear that Isaac, agonizingly aware that he was tricked and that Esau was defrauded, is bound by a system that makes it impossible to revoke the blessing he gave Jacob. Like an entry in a ship's log or a surgeon who amputates the wrong leg, there's no do-over or going back to fix things. Undoing a blessing is as impossible as "unbaptizing" someone.

What are the implications of this sorry tale of deceit for us today? Perhaps the main one is to learn from Esau's previously cavalier dismissal of his birthright: "Then Jacob gave Esau bread and pottage of lentiles; and he did eat and drink, and rose up, and went his way: thus Esau despised his birthright."[117]

This verse doesn't use the wording "a mess of pottage," with *mess* meaning a meal, and *pottage* meaning a stew. Nor does the phrase *mess of pottage* appear anywhere in the *King James Version*. Yet the phrase has long been used to highlight the value Esau placed on his birthright, as defined in the Wikipedia entry on *Mess of Pottage*. It describes the concept as follows: "A mess of pottage is something immediately attractive but of little value taken foolishly and carelessly in exchange for something more distant and perhaps less tangible but immensely more valuable."

And there lies the most important lesson we can discern today: We are to prize and cherish blessings that are not yet ours but which

---

[115] Genesis 27:31-35.
[116] Genesis 27:20.
[117] Genesis 25:34 (*King James Version*).

we can anticipate in the future. For example, a student in med school can reasonably anticipate graduation and a job practicing as a doctor. Someone in their 50s can reasonably anticipate retirement in a decade or so. While none of these future states is guaranteed, they have good reason to believe they have a good future ahead of them. Similarly, while neither Jacob nor Esau were guaranteed to receive their father's blessing (he could have died unexpectedly before awarding it), they could reasonably expect they would receive his blessing.

There's a concept in the world of finance that has something of a parallel to us anticipating future blessings. It's called "future value." This is what you anticipate the value of a current asset will be at some future date. This is based on an assumed rate of growth, for example at 5 percent interest. This last part of the definition doesn't concern us, but the concept of something's future value does. As a famished young man, desperate for some of his brother's stew, he casually ignored the future value of the blessing that he knew would one day should have been his. What folly.

24

A Blessing Demanded

So Jacob was left alone, and a man wrestled with him till daybreak. When the man saw that he could not overpower him, he touched the socket of Jacob's hip so that his hip was wrenched as he wrestled with the man. Then the man said, "Let me go, for it is daybreak." But Jacob replied, "I will not let you go unless you bless me."

— Genesis 32:24-26.

What right do we have to demand anything of God, or His representative (in the case, perhaps an angel)? Clearly, Jacob thought he was entitled to a blessing after his prolonged bout with this mysterious, but undoubtedly divine, stranger. Somehow, he knew this was no ordinary human encounter with some belligerent Bedouin, perhaps. Something about the battle made it plain that this was a spiritual ordeal, one that left him with a dislocated hip.

Then came the blessing itself, in the form of a new name. His opponent announced: "Your name will no longer be Jacob, but Israel, because you have struggled with God and with humans and have overcome."[118] His new name probably means "he struggles with God."

What about us? Few of us are going to have anything comparable to the experience of the man Israel (the patriarch formerly known as Jacob). If we haven't already, it may be that we have some profound

---

[118] Genesis 32:28.

spiritual encounter with God. However, it's almost certainly something that God will initiate, not something which He gives us because we demand it.

The same applies to material blessings. Let's look at the prayer of Jabez, an otherwise obscure fellow whose prayer recorded in 1 Chronicles became the object of a best-selling book some years ago: "Jabez cried out to the God of Israel, 'Oh, that you would bless me and enlarge my territory! Let your hand be with me, and keep me from harm so that I will be free from pain.' And God granted his request."[119]

His name apparently means pain, and some commentators think his name is associated with the difficulty his mother had giving birth to him. That's why part of his prayer is that God would keep him free from pain. Yet our focus is on his request that God will "enlarge my territory." How appropriate is that request? And is it a request of the same order as Jacob's demand for a blessing? There's a difference between a demand ("Hey buddy, hand over your wallet!") and a request ("Say, buddy, can you spare me a dollar?").

How do we assess the motive and the context of the one requesting (or demanding) a blessing? J. Oswald Sanders is helpful here. Commenting on Jabez's prayer, he says: "Our ambition [or prayer or request] should be for a wider influence for God, a deeper love toward God, a strong faith in God and a growing knowledge of God. The motive of our ambition must be carefully watched, but when it is right, God will not deny our prayer for an enlarged sphere.... There is nothing which God will not do for the man whose sole ambition is for His greater glory."[120]

There's the key. If our goal arises from pure, God-pleasing motives, and with a view to advancing God's kingdom (as best we can understand it), then seeking a blessing seems perfectly in order. We understand that Jacob's encounter with God was a deeply spiritual episode. We can therefore assume he demanded a blessing to equip him for what lay ahead in his role as one destined to carry Abraham's mantle on behalf of God's chosen people.

---

[119] 1 Chronicles 4:10.
[120] J. Oswald Sanders, *Problems of Christian Discipleship*, p. 91.

We know virtually nothing about Jabez. He is such an obscure figure that he doesn't even rate a mention in some Bible dictionaries. While in general we should be cautious about demanding anything of God, think for a moment of the daring claim made by Meister Eckhart (1260-1328), a German theologian and mystic: "… finding thee ready [God] is obliged to act, to overflow into thee; just as the sun must needs burst forth when the air is bright and clear and is unable to contain itself." He is saying that if we are ready to serve God, God in turn *must of necessity* respond and bless us. The notion that we can at times *oblige* God to act, if you agree with Eckhart, is astonishing. Perhaps a more manageable idea is that by His very nature, God *chooses* to bless, out of the abundance of His grace and love. Unlike Jacob the wrestler, we don't have to fight for God's blessings. We just need to extend our hands to receive them.

25

Jesus Blesses the Children

Your children are the greatest gift God will give to you, and their souls the heaviest responsibility He will place in your hands. Take time with them, teaching them to have faith in God. Be a person in whom they can have faith. When you are old, nothing else you've done will have mattered as much.

—*Lisa Wingate*[121]

As noted in the **Introduction**, when our children were young, we'd read them a Bible story at bedtime, tuck them in and say this prayer: "God bless Sarah and Matthew, and keep them safe, and well, and happy."

Not having Jesus on hand, blessing them in person was the best we could do. But it raises the question: What might Jesus have said when blessing the children? Let's review the event, as Mark records it:

People were bringing little children to Jesus for him to place his hands on them, but the disciples rebuked them. When Jesus saw this, he was indignant. He said to them, "Let the little children come to me, and do not hinder them, for the kingdom of God belongs to such as these. Truly I tell you, anyone who will not receive the kingdom of God like a little child will never enter it." And he took the children in his arms, placed his hands on them and blessed them.[122]

---

[121] Quoted in Gordon S. Jackson, *You've Made Your Bed, Now Go Bounce on It: 800 Quotes About Children, Their Parents and Others Who Care About Them.*
[122] Mark 10:14-16.

One thing to note is that this is the only instance of apparently "unneedy" people getting Jesus' attention, blessing or healing. Elsewhere we read how He heals the lepers, the blind, or the paralyzed. Or He probes the spiritual needs of Nicodemus or the rich young ruler, all of them people who have come to Hm of their own accord, wanting something from Him—if not a blessing per se, at least some of His wisdom. But not with the children. Their parents brought them to Jesus, not because their young lives were marred with leprosy, blindness or paralysis, or because they had deep theological issues they wanted to pursue with this rabbi. Nor, from what we can tell, had they come for any teaching. There's no evidence that Jesus hauled out a flannel board and gave them the kiddy-version of the Good Samaritan.

Rather, all they brought was themselves, and in so doing gave Jesus two teaching opportunities for another audience: His well-intentioned but yet-again-misguided disciples who tried to protect Jesus from these little people. The first was to emphasize to the disciples how beloved and welcome these children were. Jesus' response to the disciples is uncharacteristically harsh, reflective of how strongly He feels about including the children in His ministry. As *The Message* puts it, "The disciples shooed them off. But Jesus was irate and let them know it."

The second lesson for the disciples was the need to focus on the children's character and qualities, for unless people "receive the kingdom of God like a little child" they will never enter it. And what are those childlike qualities that made Jesus so ready to bless these children? A simplicity, trust, humility, total dependence on others, spontaneity, and an openness to learning. Jesus is in effect saying that only those who accept the kingdom of God as a gift will enter it. Clearly, these children were drawn to Jesus and were utterly comfortable with Him, ready to be taken in His arms.

One commentary says, "The receptiveness of these children was a great contrast to the stubbornness of the religious leaders, who let their education and sophistication stand in the way of the simple faith needed to believe in Jesus; and the dullness of the disciples, whose self-centeredness continued to blind them to Jesus' true mission. No wonder Jesus used children as an example for hard-hearted adults."[123]

What did He say in blessing these children? We don't know. But the Greek verb "is intensive in force, suggesting that his blessing was fervent. The verb is also in the imperfect tense, meaning that he kept on blessing. Jesus took time with each child, blessing each as he or she was brought to him."[124]

Jesus' readiness to welcome the children, and His emphasis on how their qualities exemplified the simplicity needed to enter God's kingdom, were in stark contrast to the prevailing view of how children were regarded. As the *Jerome Commentary* notes, "In writings of the time, children are presented as either examples of unreasonable behavior or objects to be trained. In this passage, they are taken seriously as persons and enjoy a relationship with Jesus and the kingdom."[125]

Despite how society may have seen them, Jesus was drawn to these young people and their childlike qualities. What baggage have we adults accumulated along the way that has smothered or squeezed out the childlike qualities we once had? Our capacity for receiving God's blessings may hinge in part on our commitment, instead of growing up, to go in the opposite direction.

---

[123] *Life Application Bible Commentary*, p. 287.
[124] *Life Application Bible Commentary*, p. 287.
[125] *The New Jerome Biblical Commentary*, p. 618

26

Blessed Bananas

Blessed are thou, Jehovah our God, King of the universe, who bringest forth bread from the earth.

— A Jewish grace

Jesus then took the loaves, gave thanks, and distributed to those who were seated as much as they wanted. He did the same with the fish.

— John 6:11

Without food, we're dead. If there's anything we should be grateful for, it's breakfast, lunch and dinner. If ever there was a blessing bestowed on us, it's God's provision of the daily nourishment we need. We in turn ought to be only too ready to bless the meal before us. Or the sandwich eaten at our desk at work. Or the mystery meat in the school cafeteria.

Yet most of the time, we take our food for granted, much like the air we breathe. Maybe we make a special effort at Thanksgiving and Christmas, perhaps Easter as well. Blessing our food, though, raises a host of questions, ranging from the substantive to the trivial. Among them are:

- Should we say a blessing, or grace, at every meal? Aren't we in danger of becoming legalistic or routine? Or is even a routine prayer better than no prayer?
- Should we say a blessing when we are sharing a meal with non-Christians? OK if it's in our home, but not in theirs?

- Should we say a blessing if we're eating in a restaurant? If so, how do we time it if we don't want the server to interrupt us? Or what if someone in the group has already started eating? Is it worth embarrassing him or her?

- What about snacks? A blessing over a banana or a power bar?

No doubt you can think of more. Maybe we need to follow the example of a pastor we knew, who with a nice sense of irony, lived by a rule to prevent his family from being ruled by rules: "If you need a fork, you say grace; otherwise not." That's not a bad idea. Whenever a fork is called for, so is a prayer. That means you're regularly reminded of the need to recognize the blessing of God's provision. But you don't succumb to a slavish and perhaps eventually mindless ritual.

It's impossible to know how Jesus approached this issue of saying grace. We know from the gospels that food featured prominently in the various accounts of His life. He was repeatedly recorded as eating with sinners, meals that greatly irritated the Jewish mucky-mucks. We also read in each of the gospels how Jesus gave thanks before the miraculous mass feedings, of the 5,000 and the 4,000. Then there was the most solemn of meals, the last supper itself. In each of the synoptic gospels, we read that Jesus blessed both the wine and the bread, giving thanks for each.

While it's plain that Jesus gave a blessing over these "special occasion" meals, what about the countless others he ate? We can't know for sure but we can safely say two things. As an observant Jew, He certainly would have been mindful of the kind of Jewish grace quoted above. Then, as the Son of God Himself, He would have had a divinely inspired "gratitude consciousness" about every aspect of His life, including food. No doubt He was aware more than any of us just how much His breathing, walking, waking, and eating were all contingent on God's grace. So it is no coincidence that in the Lord's prayer, He specifically points to the dependence we have on God the Father when it comes to our daily bread.

The point is that we bless God out of thanks or praise, or bless our fellow humans. As we noted in **Blessings are for People and not Things**, we need to beware that we don't attribute blessedness to objects in the sense that they now have some magical or special power. When we bless a house, a ship, or a meal, or consecrate a church, a cross, or a rosary, we are seeking God's grace and goodwill on the people who will use those items.

Enter theologian Anthony Thiselton, who has a grumble. It's about the *King James Version's* translation of a verse describing the last supper. The verse in question is, "Jesus took bread, and blessed it, and brake it."[126] Actually, it's more than just a grumble: "The *KJV* most unfortunately, if not tragically," he says, translates the verse by emphasizing that Jesus blessed the *bread*, rather than blessing or thanking *God.* "Yet the Jewish haggadah[127] of the passion meal explicitly states that the host blesses God for the bread. 'Bless' applies to God in praise and thanks, not to the bread, still less to some supposed 'consecration,' as this has passed into much of church tradition." The blessing was focused on God Himself, not on the meal. Thiselton adds, "A Jew of the time would know that Jesus said 'grace,' that is, blessed *God* for the loaves...."[128]

Would Jesus have said grace over a banana? Or followed the fork rule? We can't know. But perhaps a clue emerges from a prayer by John Calvin to be said after a meal:

> *We give thanks, O God and Father, for the many mercies which you constantly bestow upon us. In supplying the food and drink necessary to sustain our present life, you show how much you care for our mortal bodies. And in supplying the life and the teachings of your Son, you reveal how much you love our immortal souls. Let the meal which we have enjoyed be a reminder to us of the eternal joy you promise to all who feed on your holy Word.*[129]

Whatever Jesus' thoughts and practices were regarding blessings at mealtimes, we can be confident that they fitted into the understanding that Calvin had of food: it was to be seen in a broader

---

[126] Matthew 26:26 (*King James Version*).

[127] The haggadah is the Jewish order of service setting out the Passover meal.

[128] Anthony Thiselton, *The Thiselton Companion to Christian Theology*, p. 153.

[129] Quoted in Robert van de Weyer, *The Fount Book of Prayer*, p. 78.

context, of a gracious God profoundly concerned with both our physical and spiritual wellbeing.

In the light of that far more comprehensive picture, somehow rules about forks and blessings over bananas seem like, well, small potatoes.

27

The "Blessed Experience"

Honor Gilbert, writing about the value of keeping a spiritual journal, described a man who went overboard, so fixated on one entry that he kept trying to re-live what for him was a spiritually profound moment. He wrote down a vivid account of his experience, and frequently re-read it and fixated on it. Then, Gilbert writes, "One day he rushed down to his wife in great distress, 'The mice have eaten my blessed experience,' he cried."[130]

This poor man had three problems. First, he kept looking backwards in his faith, not forward. He should have heeded the wisdom of Paul Tournier, who said, "The Holy Spirit is always calling us to look forward, not back."[131] Blessings await, as that beloved passage in Lamentations notes, "Because of the Lord's great love we are not consumed, for his compassions never fail. They are new every morning; great is your faithfulness."[132]

We shouldn't be living out our faith journey with our eyes constantly on the rear-view mirror. Yes, learning from and building

---

[130] Edward England, *Keeping a Spiritual Journal*, p. 150.
[131] Paul Tournier, *The Adventure of Living*, p. 40.
[132] Lamentations 3:22-23.

upon our experiences of God is crucial as we move toward Christian maturity. But this poor fellow went beyond looking in the mirror; he had turned his car around to see where he'd come from.

Second, his was a self-absorbed faith, focusing on *his* experience, and what God had done for *him.* He was living out a Christian experience so narrowly defined that he precluded whatever else God had in store for him. He had done exactly what Oswald Chambers warned against: "not to make a fetish of your rare moments."[133]

The third problem was getting rid of the mice.

---

[133] Oswald Chambers, *My Utmost for His Highest*, April 25.

28

Jesus the Blessed

Those who went ahead and those who followed shouted,
"Hosanna!"
"Blessed is he who comes in the name of the Lord!"
"Blessed is the coming kingdom of our father David!"
"Hosanna in the highest heaven!"

—Mark 11:9-10

When we think of Jesus' miracles, we recall His healing of the sick or lame, restoring sight to the blind, or even raising the dead. But a miracle involving punctuation? Well, if not a miracle, we're talking about what is at least a major transformation: from a question mark to an exclamation point.

Halford Luccock says that preceding Jesus' entry into Jerusalem, "Jesus had often been greeted with a question mark. His neighbors at Nazareth put a large question mark beside Him: 'Where did this man get all this?' John the Baptist did much the same thing: 'Are you he who is to come, or shall we look for another?' And Pilate: 'So you are a king?' The world has had its millions of question marks about Jesus...."[134] But then, Luccock continues, with Jesus' triumphal entry, those questions are blown away by a crowd who recognize at least part of His uniqueness, questions that are replaced with exclamation marks.

---

[134] *The Interpreter's Bible*, volume 7, p. 826.

No, there weren't any punctuation marks in the Greek manuscripts of the New Testament. Yet many, if not most, recent English translations add an exclamation mark after *Hosanna* to capture the intensity of the crowd's feelings. The *Expanded Bible* is especially helpful here, with the comment it includes on the word *hosanna* and its meaning: "Praise God! [Hosanna! A Hebrew word originally used in praying for help, but by this time a joyful shout of praise to God.]"

Luccock says that "an exclamation point is the only possible punctuation for this word of praise [Hosanna] and salutation." The reason, he says, is that "When we follow him, when we do the things that he says, our punctuation marks change. It is no longer 'Are you?' but 'Hosanna!'"[135]

Which raises the question, Why *Hosanna*? Why this word of praise and salutation? The answer lies in the "double blessedness" that Mark notes: Jesus' blessed status and the blessedness of "the coming kingdom."[136] Ironically, even though those individuals acclaimed Jesus as ushering in what they assumed was an earthly kingdom, as the *African Bible Commentary* notes, "Little did they realize that what they were praying for was in the process of being fulfilled"[137]—that is, God's *true* kingdom was being ushered in.

Our focus here, however, is on Jesus and His blessedness. Why does the crowd see Him as blessed and what is their justification for doing so? Our answers have their roots in Psalm 118:26: "Blessed is he who comes in the name of the Lord." This excerpt is from one of what are known as the Hallel psalms, compositions sung at festival times and during Passover. As the *African Bible Commentary* adds, "These words took on a new meaning in the New Testament when Jesus, in a way beyond all others, came 'in the name of the Lord' and offered himself as a sacrifice there in Jerusalem."[138]

We now see Jesus as God incarnate, who gave Himself on the cross for our sins—an understanding that the welcoming crowd that

---

[135] *The Interpreter's Bible*, volume 7, p. 827.
[136] Matthew's account of Jesus' entry into Jerusalem omits the reference to the coming kingdom.
[137] *African Bible Commentary*, p. 1190.
[138] *African Bible Commentary*, p. 721.

day could not yet have fully grasped. He was thus blessed in two ways. One, as the Son of God Himself, He was by definition blessed and worthy of praise. His divine status commanded and demanded our praise and honor, as the crowd showered on Him that day—although, as we have seen, they did so with only a limited understanding of His true identity or of the magnitude of what the cross would imply. He was worthy of those palm branches and cloaks spread out in homage. In addition, He was blessed in the sense of what He would accomplish. He made it possible for us to be reconciled with God, paralleling what Jesus had taught about the prodigal son and his father.

In other words, Jesus enabled us to be welcomed home. No question about it.

29

Bless me Father, for I have Sinned

Protestants have something to learn from their Catholic friends about the blessing that results from confession[139] of their sins. Depending on their tradition, Protestants may include a time for confession during worship services. It's said as a congregation, perhaps as part of a written liturgy. The United Methodist Church, for instance, states the following on its website:

> While The United Methodist Church does not consider confession a sacrament, we know our need to confess our sin before God and one another. As they gather for worship, United Methodists often offer a prayer of confession. Through spoken prayer and a time of silent prayer, we confess our sinfulness before God. The confession should be followed by a declaration of pardon. Confession and pardon together remind us that we are sinners saved by grace.[140]

Whatever the benefits of corporate confession, and clearly they are significant, they lack the one-on-one, personalized confession that Catholics make to a priest. To assess the nature of the blessing that

---

[139] *Confession* is used in Christian thinking in two ways: here, in the sense of admitting one's sins as part of our repentance, and in the sense of affirming our faith. This latter usage includes affirming certain statements of faith, like the Apostles Creed, the Augsburg Confession of Faith, the Nicene Creed and the Westminster Confession of Faith.

[140] https://www.resourceumc.org/en/content/to-be-united-methodist-why-do-we-have-prayers-of-confession-in-worship.

accompanies confession, let's look at the steps this entails. It begins with the penitent saying, "Bless me Father, for I have sinned." Then, as prescribed by the Roman Catholic church's Rite of Penance, the penitent says, "It has been [insert an amount of time] since my last confession. For these and all the sins of my past life, I am truly sorry."

All mortal sins, those that in the Church's teaching would lead to damnation if not confessed, must then be shared with the priest. Confession of venial sins is recommended but not required. These sins are not as serious but still lead to a weakening of the person's relationship with God. Having heard the confession, the priest assigns a penance, possibly a prayer of contrition, and then proclaims, "I absolve you from your sins in the name of the Father, and of the Son, and of the Holy Spirit."[141]

Finally, the priest invites the penitent to "give thanks to the Lord, for he is good" and the penitent responds, "His mercy endures forever." The encounter concludes with the priest dismissing the penitent "in peace."

Most Protestants wouldn't object to anyone confessing to a priest. However, despite a wide range of Protestant views on the subject, they would most likely deny that confessing to a priest is *necessary*. They would point to Paul's word to Timothy: "For there is one God and one mediator between God and mankind, the man Christ Jesus...."[142]

In a thoughtful paper titled "Why Go to Confession,"[143] Fr. John Flader, an Australian priest, notes several benefits—or we could call them blessings—that arise from what Catholics regard as the sacrament of confession. Flader writes that confession leads to the blessing of knowing we are forgiven. When the priest, acting on Christ's behalf, says "I absolve you," Flader adds, "We need to hear

---

[141] Or the priest may use a longer form: "God, the Father of mercies, through the death and resurrection of his Son has reconciled the world to himself and sent the Holy Spirit among us for the forgiveness of sins. Through the ministry of the Church may God give you pardon and peace. And I absolve you from your sins in the name of the Father, and of the Son, and of the Holy Spirit."

[142] 1 Timothy 2:5.

[143] chrome-extension://efaidnbmnnnibpcajpcglclefindmkaj/https://irp-cdn.multiscreensite.com/7fe73157/files/uploaded/Why-Go-to-Confession.pdf

those words with our ears, and only then are we certain that we are forgiven.... Our Lord instituted the sacraments [including confession] as outward signs precisely so that we could know when grace is acting in us." It's crucial to emphasize that in Catholic teaching, the priest is not forgiving the penitent; only God forgives sins. Rather, the priest, acting as God's agent, is declaring that God has indeed forgiven the penitent following what is assumed to be a sincere confession.

Additional benefits from confession include the need to examine our conscience beforehand, thus forcing us to know ourselves better, "to see where we have failed since our last confession and where we repeatedly fail." This step also leads to greater self-knowledge and growth in humility, Flader writes. But the most important blessing is of course the forgiveness of our sins and the gift of God's grace to us.

Let us leave aside the objections Protestants may have to Catholic or Orthodox theology surrounding confessions and focus on the issue at hand: the blessing that confession affords the penitent. For, as Flader writes, "confession gives us a new beginning in the spiritual struggle."

We leave with a clean slate. Christians of all traditions can thus agree with author Ada Lum's observation: "I like sunrises, Mondays, and new seasons. God seems to be saying, 'with me you can always start afresh.'"[144]

---

[144] Quoted in *Encounter with God* Scripture Union Bible reading notes. Date unknown.

30

Blessings as Prayers

We may encounter two types of blessing when next we go to worship: those directed at God, and those directed toward us. As we've noted elsewhere, when we say we're "blessing" God, we're talking about praising and honoring Him. Again, we'll refer to Psalm 103, which in the *King James Version* begins with *bless*. Other more modern versions typically use *praise*.

Bless the Lord, O my soul: and all that is within me, bless his holy name.

Bless the Lord, O my soul, and forget not all his benefits:

Who forgiveth all thine iniquities; who healeth all thy diseases;

Who redeemeth thy life from destruction; who crowneth thee with lovingkindness and tender mercies;

Who satisfieth thy mouth with good things; so that thy youth is renewed like the eagle's.[145]

The other category of blessing consists of invocations or benedictions during worship. But there's no reason you couldn't pray these blessings yourself, during your private devotions, applying them to your own situation.[146] The emphasis in the six blessings presented here lend themselves both to private and corporate worship. Some are familiar, others less so.

---

[145] Psalm 103:1-6 (*King James Version*).
[146] The entry titled **Saying Goodbye—Benedictions and Doxologies**, overlaps with this one.

Gordon S. Jackson

The Lord Jesus Christ be near to defend thee, within thee to refresh thee, around thee to preserve thee, before thee to guide thee, behind thee to justify thee, above thee to bless thee; who liveth and reigneth with the Father and the Holy Spirit, God for evermore.

—*Anonymous, 10th century*

Unto God's gracious mercy and protection we commit you. The Lord bless you and keep you. The Lord make his face to shine upon you and be gracious to you. The Lord lift his countenance upon you, and give you peace.

—*The Aaronic blessing*[147]

May God in the plenitude of his love pour upon you the torrents of his grace, bless you and keep you in his holy fear, prepare you for a happy eternity, and receive you at last into immortal glory.

—*Blessing at the Consecration of Coventry Cathedral, England*

May God free you, may God guard you night and day.
May God set you in your right place, and may you spread out like the grass of a prairie.
Spread out like palm leaves; continue your walk, and may life be with you.
May God place you where God's stars are placed at dawn and at night.
Spread out like water of a lake.
Be numerous like the feet of a millipede.

—*Kenyan blessing*

---

[147] Numbers 6:24-26.

May the road rise to meet you.
May the wind be always at your back.
May the sunshine warm upon your face.
May the rains fall softly upon your fields until we meet again.
May God hold you in the hollow of his hand.

—Old Gaelic blessing

May the love of the Lord Jesus
Draw us to himself;
May the power of the Lord Jesus
Strengthen us in his service;
May the joy of the Lord Jesus
Fill our souls.
May the blessing of God almighty,
The Father, the Son, and the Holy Ghost,
Be amongst you
And remain with you
Always.

—William Temple

31

Blessed be the Name of the Lord

*Job got up and tore his robe and shaved his head. Then he fell to the ground
in worship and said:*
"Naked I came from my mother's womb,
*and naked I will depart. The Lord gave and the Lord has taken away; may
the name of the Lord be praised."*
—Job 1:20-21

The *New International Version*, cited here, is an outlier in the way it
presents the last line of verse 21. Most translations have,
"Blessed be the name of the Lord." Either way, Job's stunning
assertion of trust in the face of all he has experienced is testimony to a
profound faith in God, *no matter what.*

With God as his foundation, the One whom he will bless
regardless of the tragedies that have befallen him, Job embraces a "no-
matter-what" kind of faith. Astonishing though it is, his example is not
the only one found in Scripture. There's the largely overlooked minor
prophet Habakkuk, who prepares his country for the inevitable
onslaught of the notoriously brutal Chaldeans by proclaiming:

Even if the fig tree does not blossom,
And there is no fruit on the vines,
If the yield of the olive fails,
And the fields produce no food,
Even if the flock disappears from the fold,

And there are no cattle in the stalls,
Yet I will triumph in the Lord,
I will rejoice in the God of my salvation.[148]

In the face of total devastation, comparable to what we saw in Ukraine cities in 2022, this man's faith enables him to assert a no-matter-what blessing of God.

How much more, then, should those of us living lives far more comfortable and trouble-free than Job or Habakkuk be praising or blessing our Lord. We should echo the words of the psalmist, who said: "I will extol thee, my God, O king; and I will bless thy name for ever and ever. Every day will I bless thee; and I will praise thy name for ever and ever."[149]

It's not only we humans who sing God's praises; so did the angels at Jesus' birth: "At once the angel was joined by a huge angelic choir singing God's praises: Glory to God in the heavenly heights, Peace to all men and women on earth who please him."[150]

Now, it's up to us to join in the music that drowns out any "no-matter-what" circumstances life has thrown our way.

---

[148] Habakkuk 3:17-18 (*New American Standard Bible*).
[149] Psalm 145:1-2 (*King James Version*).
[150] Luke 2:13 (*The Message*).

32

Blessings Unexpected, Blessings Undeserved

[David] was not willing to take the ark of the Lord to be with him in the City of David. Instead, he took it to the house of Obed-Edom the Gittite. The ark of the Lord remained in the house of Obed-Edom the Gittite for three months, and the Lord blessed him and his entire household.
—2 Samuel 6:10-11

If Obed-Edom were around today, he'd probably be minding his own business, watching ESPN or changing the oil in his Ford 150 pickup when along comes King David. And the King is not in a good mood. As the preceding verses tell us, the journey of the ark towards Jerusalem was disrupted by the shock of Uzzah's death. This event mars what is intended to be a great triumphal political and religious victory. Uzzah was the poor fellow who had good intentions of steadying the ark when the oxen carrying it stumbled. God wasn't pleased with this non-priest touching the sacred object, and he drops dead as a result.

The mystery of God's apparent harshness isn't our concern, though. Our focus is on this otherwise obscure Obed-Edom, who is mentioned only here in the Bible (and in the parallel account of these events in 1 Chronicles 13). The man rises to prominence simply because his house happened to be on the route the ark was taking to Jerusalem. Given what had happened to Uzzah, David decides to leave the ark with a man who was apparently a Philistine from Gath.

Matthew Henry points out that Obed-Edom must have been aware of Uzzah's death, and what would have engendered a sobering, if not terrifying, sense of the ark's power. Even though Obed-Edom saw that "David himself was afraid of meddling with it, yet he [Obed-Edom] opens his door to it without fear." He then plays host to the ark for three months. Then comes the unexpected: "…and the Lord blessed him and his entire household." Henry observes, "It is good living in a family that entertains the ark, for all about it will fare the better for it."[151]

How are Obed-Edom and his household blessed? And why them? First, let's note that the man doesn't have the right pedigree to be a keeper of the ark; he is a Philistine. Admittedly, he was presumably one of the Philistines loyal to David and obviously well enough accepted by the Israelites that David felt comfortable leaving the ark in his care.

And why him? God sends blessings on whomever He wishes. Whether any of his neighbors had blessing-envy, we don't know. But in God's playing out of events, Obed-Edom was the man to whom He turned, for reasons we cannot know.

Obed-Edom's experience is reflected in the wisdom of William Wilberforce's observation, when that great anti-slavery crusader wrote, "How little do you know to what services Providence may call you."[152] So here was Providence appointing a Philistine as an unlikely keeper of Israel's most valued religious symbol.

We too cannot know to what tasks God may without warning steer our way. Nor should we raise an eyebrow of disapproval when God brings into His purposes someone who's not a member of our club. ("Come on David, couldn't you find anyone from the tribe of Judah to take on this self-storage role for a while?")

Then there's the blessing itself. What form did it take? Did his crops have a bumper yield during those three months? Did his wife give birth to twins? Did he win the Jerusalem Powerball Lottery three months in a row?

---

[151] *Matthew Henry's Commentary* (1 volume), p. 334.
[152] *365 Days With Wilberforce*, ed. Kevin Belmonte, Feb. 29.

Again, we don't know. But it was clear enough that this blessing not only came to David's attention, but it also reaffirmed his faith in the ark and its ability to bless. So he initiates the final steps of the ark's journey and brings it to Jerusalem.

And what of Obed-Edom's situation after the ark moved on to Jerusalem? Maybe the undisclosed blessings continued to ripple through his household long into the future. But we can be sure that whatever the blessings were, they were significant enough to make it into the biblical record.

The Anglican Church in Egypt has a two-campus theological college, based jointly in Cairo and Alexandria. The school began in 2005 and its founding document said it aspired to produce graduates who lived "in anticipation of miracle and acceptance of constraint." The arrival of the ark in Obed-Edom's life was something of a miracle, with the unexpected blessing it brought to him and his family. That kind of unexpectedness should leave us too in perpetual anticipation of miracles, living in the unhesitating confidence that at any moment, God could bring a miracle to bear on our circumstances. Simultaneously, though, we ought also to live with the "acceptance of constraint" of a real world, marked today by the ordinary, the routine, the predictable—watching ESPN or changing the oil.

33

Blessings in Bad Times

Horatio Gates Spafford was a nineteenth-century lawyer in Chicago who encountered a string of tragedies that sorely tested his faith. The first was in 1871, with the Great Fire of Chicago, which destroyed his investment in property in the city. Serious though that was, the second tragedy was far more devastating. The family planned a vacation to England, for Spafford, his wife Anna, and their four daughters. Spafford had to change his plans at the last minute because of legal issues arising from the fire two years before and Anna and the children went on ahead.

Their ship collided with another vessel, resulting in the loss of 226 lives—including all four of the Spafford daughters. Anna alone survived and upon arriving in England sent her husband the haunting telegram, "Saved alone."

Later, the Spaffords had three more children, one of whom died at the age of three from scarlet fever. But it was the loss of the four girls that led Spafford, while sailing across the Atlantic to rejoin Anna after the tragedy, to write the hymn for which he is now known. Here is the first verse:

When peace, like a river, attendeth my way,
When sorrows like sea billows roll;
Whatever my lot, thou has taught me to say,
It is well, it is well with my soul.

It is astonishing that someone who suffered such a grievous loss could write that "It is well, it is well with my soul." Such acceptance of the horror of losing his four daughters reflects a faith with deep, deep roots. That his soul is blessed with peace and acceptance, in the wake of this loss, and his ability to look forward rather than back, is captured in a later verse, which goes:

But Lord, 'tis for Thee, for Thy coming we wait,
The sky, not the grave, is our goal;
Oh, trump of the angel! Oh, voice of the Lord!
Blessed hope, blessed rest of my soul.

J. Oswald Sanders quotes a friend who said the following about the prospect of something bad happening: "The Lord may not have planned that this should overtake me, but he has most certainly permitted it. Therefore, though it were an attack of the enemy, by the time it reaches me, it has the Lord's permission and therefore all is well. He will make it work together with all life's experiences for good."[153]

Now, two questions. Whatever your circumstances, are you able to assert that "It is well, it is well with my soul?" (And perhaps especially if you *are* facing some grievous loss, can you still say those words?) Then, what is possibly a brutal question, if these words don't come easily or not at all, ask, "Why, exactly, is it *not* well with my soul?" Your answer may prod you to a new depth of faith, and a state of blessedness, you didn't know was possible.

---

[153] J. Oswald Sanders, *Every Life a Plan of God*, p. 105.

34

A Blessing Abused

The Ziphites went up to Saul at Gibeah and said, "Is not David hiding among us in the strongholds at Horesh, on the hill of Hakilah, south of Jeshimon? Now, Your Majesty, come down whenever it pleases you to do so, and we will be responsible for giving him into your hands." Saul replied, "The Lord bless you for your concern for me. Go and get more information. Find out where David usually goes and who has seen him there. They tell me he is very crafty. Find out about all the hiding places he uses and come back to me with definite information. Then I will go with you; if he is in the area, I will track him down among all the clans of Judah."
—*1 Samuel 23:19-23.*

This is one of the saddest passages in the Old Testament, where we see a relentless, and increasingly deranged, King Saul seeking to hunt down David. We also have the Ziphites, members of the tribe of Judah, eager to win Saul's favor by helping in his quest. In addition to his favor, they receive his blessing: "The Lord bless you for your concern for me."

What a bogus blessing: A murderous king, conniving with some opportunistic allies in the campaign to kill a young rebel who has that status only because of Saul's paranoia. Blessing people who want to see an innocent man captured and no doubt executed? Saul compounds the offense by calling on the name of the Lord to show favor to the

Ziphites, the Lord from whom Israel's first monarch is now increasingly alienated.

Why the Ziphites were ready to betray David isn't clear. We know he was hiding in their territory and perhaps with his band of men, they were proving to be an uncomfortable or disruptive presence. Here, perhaps, was their opportunity to be rid of what was in effect a guerilla gang and its leader. But whatever their motives, Saul chooses to bless them. As we have seen in our definition of *blessing*, this is a concept not to be trifled with. That is all the more so when we explicitly bless someone or something in the name of God Himself. But Saul seems to have been oblivious to the fast-and-loose approach he was taking to something sacred. Who knows, maybe it was with a touch of irony that the writer of this passage chose to include the phrase "the Lord bless you" in this report of Saul's gratitude.

What about us? While we're unlikely to be hunting down our enemies and committed to their execution, we may nevertheless at times unwittingly emulate Saul's fast-and-loose embrace of calling on the Lord, for His approval of what may be a dubious enterprise. Sometimes we get so caught up in a cause (a fight at church, a political issue, whatever) that we lose sight of the bigger picture that God would have us bear in mind. Hence, a word of caution. We should be careful what we bless. This could be something that, with some emotional distance and clear thinking, we'd agree is plainly wrong. Or it may be misguidedly seeking blessings on trivialities, such as asking God's blessing on your favorite team for the Super Bowl, that they may win.

35

A Blessing for the Hyper-Hypocrite

The scene: Moses is face to face with Pharaoh for the last time, following the horrific death of the first-born children and animals. This final plague has at last convinced Pharaoh to free the Israelites. He cannot move fast enough to be rid of Moses, Aaron and this slave-nation who have caused him and his country such suffering. He tells Moses and Aaron to leave and worship God. "Take your flocks and herds … and go," he says, before adding an odd and unexpected final word: "And also bless me."[154]

What lies behind his request? Here's one of the most powerful men on the planet, thwarted at every turn by a man who's spent half his life as a shepherd in Midian, and he's now asking Moses to bless him? Who knows; perhaps at this moment, following the death of his own son, he's finally grasped the majesty and power of the one true God, the God to whom Moses and Aaron have been appealing since their first audacious encounter with this ruler.

This is the last time he and Moses will speak and this request for a blessing is the last thing he says to Moses. Does Pharaoh assume that Moses himself is capable of blessing him, or is he calling on Moses' God to bless him, as some translations suggest? It probably makes no difference, given that we'll soon learn that this plea for a blessing is hardly a genuine "Come-to-Yahweh" moment.

---

[154] Exodus 12:32.

Maybe Pharaoh finally grasped the greatness of the Israelites' God, and his uncontested superiority over the Egyptian gods and what he regards as his own divine status. But if so, it proves to be a short-lived respect for God, as we know from his subsequent change of mind and ill-fated pursuit of his slave-labor workforce as they head to the Red Sea.

His request for a blessing is not only insincere and hypocritical, it is also vague and apparently desperate. It seems that he has no clear idea what he's seeking from Moses or God. We notice that there's no record of Moses responding. Pharaoh is grasping, hoping for something, anything good that this shepherd-leader may be able to give him—or petition his God to provide.

For a moment, we may even feel pity for this man: bereft of his firstborn, realizing his impotence against a God whose powers have repeatedly publicly humiliated him—*him*, the Pharaoh! Our pity, though, is hardly warranted, as it's clear that Pharaoh's heart hardens yet again and he changes his mind. His request for a blessing is thus a sham.

Does Pharaoh's request for a blessing hold any lessons for us? We're not in positions of power even remotely comparable to Pharaoh's. But we do need to pay attention to the context of our requests for God's blessings. This is especially if we've had a prolonged season of an unhappy relationship with God. It may be that we continue to be angry with Him after losing our job, the death of a loved one, or some other trauma. Or it may be that we're in a spiritual slump for no apparent reason or that we, like Pharaoh, have experienced a series of hardships. Perhaps we're questioning God's love and care. At such a moment, perhaps all we can do is say, "Bless me." Maybe we can't be much more specific than that. And also like Pharaoh, maybe we're recognizing that God is bigger than our problems. But if that's the case, we need to take a further step, one that

Pharaoh didn't: Believe that God will bless anyone approaching Him in good faith, with a truly repentant heart, and committed to doing His will going forward. Pharaoh went 0 for 3 on these criteria.

Whatever catastrophic situation we may have faced, whatever our context, whatever loss we may have suffered, we can call for God's blessing with the assurance that He will listen. It's also helpful if you're seeking a blessing, to answer Jesus' question, "What do you want me to do for you?" Not only will God listen, He will act, just as He did one time after another in Egypt to free His people from a man who even in his most desperate hour wouldn't recognize the one God whose blessing he supposedly sought.

PART 4

Some Matters Arising

36

Bless My Cotton Socks

When we defined *blessing* earlier we drew a distinction between hallowed and colloquial blessings. It's now time to examine the latter and their implications. Depending on the culture in which you were raised, you may well have as part of your conversation sayings like "Bless my cotton socks," "Well bless my heart!" and "Bless your lucky stars."[155]

And then there's the widespread "Bless you!" in response to a sneeze. The origins of this saying are murky. One explanation is that during a bout of the plague in Europe in the sixth century, Pope Gregory the Great encouraged people to say "God bless you" to protect people's health. Another theory is that people in the Middle Ages believed that when you sneezed, your soul was at that moment vulnerable to attack by Satan. Hence the blessing for your protection.

Regardless of the saying's origins, we can be confident that the next time a friend says "Bless you!" after you sneeze, it's unlikely that the person is seriously seeking God's hand of protection over you, to preserve you from the plague or a moment of Satanic opportunism.

Nevertheless, let's assume that God notes your friend's comment and records it in file 6930-R, the place where all "not-to-be-taken-terribly-seriously" prayers end up. Joining them are comparable

---

[155] The on-line Free Dictionary offers dozens of examples, some that we'd regard as "hallowed" blessings, but most are in the colloquial category. See https://idioms.thefreedictionary.com/bless.

utterances that flow more from habit than genuine Christian devotion. Example: "We'll be there by 7, God willing." Or taking the oath in a courtroom, just how devout are each of those folks saying, "So help me God"? Or the politician's rousing conclusion to a speech with the mandatary exit line, "God bless America." Probably most of these requests for blessings end up in file 6930-R.

Just as "Bless you" has a veneer of spirituality attached to it, so do the "God willing" that punctuates the end of sentences for some people, and the "So help me God" rattled off at the end of a swearing-in. In reality, God's divine powers have most likely not been activated in response. But if in most of these uses, nothing positive is accomplished, has any actual harm been done?

Probably not. At the very least, though, a habit like "Bless you" is indicative of a thoughtless trifling with things that have something of the sacred about them. It's like using a piece of the family silver for your dog's water bowl. No actual harm will result. But you should presumably think twice about doing that.

Let us return for a moment to the image we used earlier about blessings being like live ammunition, to be handled with great respect and in an awareness of their power. Maybe the colloquial use of *bless* and *blessings* is like messing with blank bullets or deactivated hand grenades. They may look like the real thing. But we know better.

37

Unpopular Blessings

Think of those for whom you seek God's blessings. You'll pray that God will meet whatever your loved ones' needs happen to be at any time: perhaps their good health, safety, academic success, financial security, and generally their overall welfare. You may pray for those beyond your circle of your immediate family and friends—perhaps acquaintances at church, the country's leaders, or medical workers dealing with COVID 19.

You are less likely to add to your list those you would define as enemies. Why would I want them to be blessed? And those who persecute me? They're deserving of curses, not blessing! Yet one of the most outrageous of Jesus' commands in the Sermon on the Mount comes immediately, and awkwardly, to mind: "But I tell you, love your enemies and pray for those who persecute you...."[156] And if that weren't enough to rattle our spiritual cages, Paul writes in Romans, "Bless those who persecute you; bless and do not curse."[157]

Think of those who have hurt you the most. Maybe it's a spouse, now pursuing divorce proceedings. Or a boss who continues to treat you with galling disrespect. Or perhaps it's the legal system, whose rules deprive you of what reasonable people would say is fair treatment. Whatever the source of the injustice, the people involved are the last ones you're inclined to pray for or to seek God's blessing.

---

[156] Matthew 5:44.
[157] Romans 12:14.

And yet…. You know what Jesus requires of you. And you're forced to come to terms with this spiritual law: If you cannot bless those on your enemies list, you're got an uncleared log jam in the river of blessings that God is sending your way.

38

Count Your Blessings, Count Them One by One

Count your many blessings, name them one by one,
And it will surprise you what the Lord hath done.
—Johnson Oatman Jr.

The British cartoon strip, Andy Capp, features a working-class layabout who never does any work. He lives off the dole (social welfare) and spends his time gambling or playing darts and snooker. He and his wife Flo live on the edge of poverty; money is always tight. That's why one of the cartoons has Flo commenting, in reference to the money in her purse, and knowing her husband's pilfering ways, that each morning she counts her blessings because they had a habit of disappearing during the night.

Then there's the hypothetical question, "What if you woke up tomorrow with only those things for which you thanked God today?" Of course, we cannot in practice thank God for every blessing we have. ("Darn, I forgot to thank Him for my hand-eye coordination. Nor did I thank Him for my gall bladder. Both gone.") No, the point isn't that there's a pouting God demanding explicit gratitude from us for all the blessings He gives us day by day. Rather, the question nudges us into a greater state of awareness and gratitude for the sea of blessings we enjoy, many of them which go unrecognized. As Matthew Henry put it, "[I]f we have been graciously preserved from blindness, and lameness, and dumbness, we have as much reason to bless God as if we had been cured."[158]

So here's a suggestion: How about listing just two blessings each day, for the coming week, for which you've never consciously thanked God before. It could be that always cheerful cashier at your grocery store, a wonderful childhood, or, yes, even your gall bladder.

Write them down. And as your list grows, you can add to your awareness of your blessings the fact that your list will never be complete.

---

[158]*Matthew Henry's Commentary* (1 volume), p. 1284.

39

Blessing Yourself—A Bad, Bad Idea

Can we bless ourselves? The possibility is raised in Moses' instructions to the Israelites when they are renewing their covenant with the Lord in the land of Moab. Here's how the *New International Version* translates the passage that interests us:

Make sure there is no man or woman, clan or tribe among you today whose heart turns away from the Lord our God to go and worship the gods of those nations; make sure there is no root among you that produces such bitter poison. When such a person hears the words of this oath and they invoke a blessing on themselves, thinking, "I will be safe, even though I persist in going my own way," they will bring disaster on the watered land as well as the dry.[159]

This notion of people invoking a blessing on themselves, for their own protection, also appears as *blessing* in the *Jerusalem Bible*. A survey of translations reveals several additional approaches. One is found in the *Amplified Bible*, which says "imagines himself as blessed." The *New American Standard Bible* has, "he will consider himself fortunate in his heart."

Regardless of the exact translation, it's plain that blessing yourself is a bad, bad idea—for at least three reasons.

One is that people seeking a self-blessing are fooling themselves, because they're going after a mirage. There's no such thing as a

---

[159] Deuteronomy 29:18-19.

blessing you initiate yourself. As we've seen throughout this book, a blessing is something done for you or given to you, by someone (or God) who has the authority to do so. It would be like giving yourself a compliment or an apology; by definition, those can come only from someone else. If you think you're blessed because of your own initiative, you need to look again at the *Amplified Bible's* wording: you are *imagining* yourself as blessed. You're living in la-la land, divorced from reality.

This leads to a second problem, arrogance. As we read above, you are in danger of thinking, as the *NIV* puts it, that "I will be safe, even though I persist in going my own way…" The implication is clearly that these people no longer see a need for God in their lives. They have become autonomous beings—and not just autonomous beings but ones who have rejected their need for the living God who brought them out of Egypt. It's as if they have said, "I'll take care of whatever blessings I need from here on; I'll manage just fine on my own." That voice of rebellion can only invite disastrous consequences, as Moses continues to say:

> *The Lord will never be willing to forgive them; his wrath and zeal will burn against them. All the curses written in this book will fall on them, and the Lord will blot out their names from under heaven. The Lord will single them out from all the tribes of Israel for disaster, according to all the curses of the covenant written in this Book of the Law.*[160]

This is harsh language… This is no nicey-nice God telling these wayward Israelites, "Who am I to judge? Have a nice day."

Part of the reason for the harshness is that God can foresee the damage these "self-blessers" would bring on their community. And that is our third reason that blessing ourselves is a bad idea. Having deluded ourselves into thinking we can get along just fine without God's leading, thank you very much, we unwittingly bring enormous harm to our community. As *The Message* puts it, we in effect tell God: "'I'll live just the way I please, thank you,' and ends up ruining life for everybody." Individual waywardness in the community of faith means

---

[160] Deuteronomy 29:20-21.

all will suffer. Paul, in his powerful analogy of the church as a body, says: "If one part suffers, every part suffers with it..."[161] Our personal sins cannot but hurt the church as a whole, and its witness to the outside world.

What may have seemed like a harmless enough idea of blessing ourselves turns out to have dire consequences, for ourselves and then rippling through our church and the wider community as well. In short, the lesson of Deuteronomy 29 is that blessing oneself is a bad idea. Better to leave the blessing we seek to God; He'll do it far better than we can.

---

[161] 1 Corinthians 12:26.

40

Blessings Forfeited

Is it possible to lose the blessings that God has given us? Yes, if the prophet Malachi is anything to go by:

"And now, you priests, this warning is for you. If you do not listen, and if you do not resolve to honor my name," says the Lord Almighty, "I will send a curse on you, and I will curse your blessings. Yes, I have already cursed them, because you have not resolved to honor me."[162]

"Curse your blessings?" Now there's an apparent paradox if ever there was one, and a sobering one as well. Here are the priests, the ones elected by God to proclaim His covenant to the people and to model it themselves—in exchange for which they can expect blessings from Yahweh himself. The Levites were set aside for priestly duties, as described in Numbers 18:8-19. God told Moses that "the Levites will be mine."[163]

Yet they were no longer honoring God and Malachi lets them have it. Hence the unexpected wording: "I will curse your blessings." This curse could apply either to the perks they received and the status they enjoyed, or it could refer to the blessings they were charged with giving God's people. Earlier in Numbers, God instructs Moses on Aaron's and the priests' role: "Tell Aaron and his sons, 'This is how you are to bless the Israelites. Say to them: 'The Lord bless you and

---

[162] Malachi 2:2.
[163] Numbers 8:14.

keep you; the Lord make His face shine on you and be gracious to you the Lord turn His face toward you and give you peace.'"[164]

Now, this blessing is rendered void because of the priests' behavior. Well, not quite yet. In the verses from Malachi cited above, note the words *warning* and *if.* There's still time to turn things around. The same applies to any of us who have somehow let our Christian witness diminish in its authenticity and impact. It's time to refurbish that witness so that our capacity to bless others is what God would have it be.

---

[164] Numbers 6:23-26.

41

Bless Us, You Know, Whatever....

Two blind men were sitting by the roadside, and when they heard that Jesus was going by, they shouted, "Lord, Son of David, have mercy on us!" The crowd rebuked them and told them to be quiet, but they shouted all the louder, "Lord, Son of David, have mercy on us!" Jesus stopped and called them. "What do you want me to do for you?" he asked. "Lord," they answered, "we want our sight." Jesus had compassion on them and touched their eyes. Immediately they received their sight and followed him.
— Matthew 20:30-34.

Note the words, "Lord, we want our sight." When Jesus asked them what they wanted and knowing His reputation as a healer who had done miracles aplenty, they called upon Him as "Lord" to restore their sight, to address a specific and easily identified need. Anticipating that this extraordinary man was capable of blessing them in an extraordinary way, they told Him precisely what they wanted. Nothing like, "Well, whatever you think would be helpful..." Or, "Just bless us, Lord; that's all we ask." No, they needed to be specific about their overwhelming need for restored sight, something obvious to them and to Jesus.

So too with Jesus' prayer in Gethsemane, when He asked His heavenly father to take away the suffering He was about to face. In anguish, Jesus was quite plain about what He wanted, while unhesitatingly deferring to the will of His Father.

The lesson for us, therefore, is that we should be as clear and concrete as possible when we ask God for those good things that we term blessings. Our prayers of petition shouldn't be vague ("Bless all the sick, Lord," or "Bring about peace throughout the world"). Instead, we should pray, "Bless the doctors who will do Uncle Jim's heart surgery on Tuesday, that their skill will help bring about his healing" or "Please give wisdom and courage to the UN peacekeepers in South Sudan as they seek to bring about stability in that country."

Think of the specificity in the Lord's prayer. In these few sentences, Jesus instructs His disciples, and us on how to use concrete language to address our heavenly Father. Imagine if, when they asked Him how to pray, He had instead said:

> *When you pray, say: "Lord, we just want to thank you, Lord, for, like, bringing us together today, Lord, and for just being who you are, Lord, and Lord, for just blessing us so much, Lord, that we like don't know how to thank you, Lord, for, like, all you've done for us, Lord, but we just praise your great and holy name, Lord and we just thank you so much, Lord, for ...."*[165]

Will God bless such a well-intentioned but all-too-vague attempt at prayer? Undoubtedly; He meets us where we are. But God knows what we truly need, like the blind men who needed to spell out their request of Jesus.

The story is told of a woman who each morning gave a one-word prayer of resignation to what the day may bring: "Whatever." Then, she'd end the day by praying, "Oh well." That's as vague as it gets. We can do better.

---

[165] This satirical prayer is excerpted from Gordon S. Jackson, *Jesus Does Standup*.

42

What of the Unblessed?

Picture the scene. You're in church with your two children. The 3-year-old has fallen asleep next to you on the pew, lying comfortably on your coat. When it's time to approach the altar for communion, you decide it's best to leave her in dreamland. But her 14-month-old brother is awake and you carry him with you as you join the communion line. You take both the wine and the bread and, following the tradition in your church, the priest or pastor says a simple blessing on your boy, and you return to your pew. You are spiritually nourished by the elements and with a blessed little boy. But what of your sleeping daughter? Will she have a less-blessed week ahead because she lost out on the words of the officiant who blessed her brother?

A silly question, perhaps. A closer look, however, suggests seemingly only one of two possibilities. One option is that the blessing the toddler received was meaningful and effected something good for the boy, and therefore his sleeping sibling lost out. Or else the blessing was an empty gesture devoid of any true benefit, and the sister didn't miss out on anything.

So, are blessings a waste of time? Time for a three-step response. First, let us consider Job and his ordeal, and how God responds to the question underlying that entire forty-two-chapter book: *Why?* Why was Job made to suffer the horrific losses that he did? God's answer beginning in chapter 38 is, strangely, to a different question altogether.

God answers the unasked question, "Do you know who you're dealing with here?" Then, having had his questioning reoriented, Job responds, "I am unworthy—how can I reply to you?" Precisely. Likewise with our question about the unblessed toddler. We are asking the wrong question; we should instead be asking, "Do you know who you're dealing with here?"

The second step is to consider the splendid book by J. B. Phillips, *Your God is Too Small*. This book, first published in 1953, essentially says that many of the questions or assumptions we have about God reflect a poor understanding of who He is. Some of the examples are now dated but the title alone should be enough to move our thinking beyond our question concerning those who are unblessed. Do we truly think of God as a churlish scorekeeper, holding a clipboard and checking off which children in your congregation were formally blessed on Sunday, and putting a red *No!* next to the name of your daughter and others who didn't make it to the front for a blessing? Or what of those others who didn't make it to church on Sunday? Are they going to have a less-than-optimal week as a result? Even asking these questions shows that we have an incomplete, shriveled view of this God whom we serve.

In another of his books, Phillips offered a useful corrective to our sometimes defective thinking about God. He writes, "Let us remind ourselves ... of the character of God, the methods of God, and the resources of God."[166] As we do so, we'll be steered away from a limited understanding of God's character, if we see him as handing out blessings only to those who are according to our legalistic mindset deserving of His grace. His methods of distributing grace and blessings are way beyond our comprehension, as is our grasp of the resources at His disposal. Let us therefore not for an instant think that the sleeping daughter was deprived of God's grace.

Our third step is to consider what God says and does regarding His willingness to bless us with His grace and forgiveness. The New Testament repeatedly indicates that God eagerly seeks to draw sinners to Himself. For example, Paul writes that God "... wants all people to

---

[166] J. B. Phillips, *Making Men Whole*, p. 26.

be saved and to come to a knowledge of the truth."[167] And John's gospel underscores God's desire: "God did not send his Son into the world to condemn the world, but to save the world through him."[168] Finally, let us look at the example of Jesus' words on the cross, to the penitent thief dying next to Him: "Jesus answered him, 'Truly I tell you, today you will be with me in paradise.'"[169]

Faced with a God who in the supreme act of love took on human form, and gave His life for us, can we still fret over whether a 3-year-old lost out over a blessing?

If so, it's time to re-read Job 38-39.

---

[167] 1 Timothy 2:4.
[168] John 3:17.
[169] Luke 23:43.

43

Blessings Deferred and the Way of the Cross

U nlike the toddler mentioned in the previous section, who missed out on a blessing in a Sunday worship service, Lazarus had a problem of a quite different magnitude. We're talking about the fellow who appears in Luke 16, in Jesus' curious parable about Lazarus and a rich man.[170] It's the only parable in which one of the characters is given a name. It's also unusual because the rich man doesn't do anything obviously wrong, yet he is punished in the afterlife.

While Jesus doesn't name him, he is traditionally referred to as *Dives*, the Latin word for a rich man. Unlike the robbers who descend on the poor victim in the Good Samaritan,[171] or the nasty judge in the parable of the persistent widow,[172] Dives is simply getting on with his life, enjoying the blessings of affluence God has apparently sent his way, without obviously harming anyone. Whether he deserves his wealth isn't clear. Nor do we know if he inherited it or gained it by exploitation of others. As Matthew Henry writes, "We cannot infer from men's living [well] that God loves them in giving them so much, or that they love God for giving them so much." He adds, "... eating good meat and wearing good clothes are lawful; but they often become

---

[170] Luke 16:19-31.
[171] Luke 10:25-37.
[172] Judges 18:2-8.

the food and fuel of pride and luxury, and so turn into sin to us."[173] Like the businessman described in the next entry, entitled **Blessings as Booty**, Dives may be guilty of hanging on to too much of what God had given him. But Jesus doesn't say.

Yet there are a couple of problems. The first concerns Dives, the second Lazarus. The first is the seemingly unfair punishment Dives receives. Yes, he enjoys his fine clothing, sumptuous meals and an affluent lifestyle. Yet in Jesus' telling of the story, he was never cruel to Lazarus. Dives didn't try to shoo him away from his gate or call the authorities to remove this unwelcome fellow who was no doubt lowering property values by his presence. (Note, by the way, that Dives was wealthy enough to have a home with a gate; he clearly lived in the better part of town.) But despite doing nothing to aggravate Lazarus' suffering, Dives ends up in torment. Why? The reason, William Barclay, says, is that Dives is the "man who never noticed."[174] Here, at his very gate day after day, a pitiful beggar lay ignored, surviving on scraps from the rich man's table. Barclay notes of Dives that his sin "was not that he did wrong things, but that he did nothing."[175]

The second problem is less easily solved. Why does God bless Dives with wealth but fail to bless Lazarus with even the most basic needs for a decent life? We do not, and cannot, know. Our first instinct might be to think of Jesus' beatitude, in which he proclaims, "Blessed are the poor," as we read in Luke's version of the beatitudes.[176] Yet to our eyes, Lazarus doesn't look the least bit blessed. Nor do we understand why he ends up in heaven while Dives doesn't. It's apparently through no merit on Lazarus' part. While the Bible repeatedly calls for a just society in which the needs of the poor, and the vulnerable like the widows and orphans, are taken care of, Scripture never glorifies poverty with a victim status that will assure one of passage into heaven.

---

[173] *Matthew Henry's Commentary*, (1 volume), p. 1475.
[174] William Barclay, *The Daily Study Bible: The Gospel of Luke*, p. 212.
[175] William Barclay, *The Daily Study Bible: The Gospel of Luke*, p. 214.
[176] Luke 6:20. Note that in Matthew's gospel Jesus speaks of the "poor in spirit." For simplicity's sake, we'll focus only on Luke's version here.

So why is Dives blessed, at least in his earthly life, and Lazarus isn't? One glib answer is the observation that if you want to know what God thinks of money, just look at who he gives it to. In this case, it's to a callous, uncaring individual who thinks beyond himself—to his five brothers—only when it's too late to do anything about his own plight. He never saw Lazarus as a fellow human being in need, let alone as anyone approaching "brother" status.

The *African Bible Commentary* says of this beggar, "All that he has going for him is the fact that he is the only person in all of Jesus' parables with a name, Lazarus. This name is the Latinized form of Eleazar and means 'God is my help.'" In a culture where names were often correlated with the character or destiny of those who bore them, Jesus' choice of Lazarus' name was no accident. The commentary continues: "Lazarus is a beggar, but he has a name. He is covered with ulcerated sores but he has human dignity. He does not remain nameless. The sin of the rich man is that he has no heart. He looks at a man with a name but does not ask him his name. He saw Lazarus' hunger and pain, but did nothing about it."[177]

Dives, though, wasn't the only one who didn't see properly. So did his fellow Jews. They drew a clear but unwarranted connection between one's affluence and God's favor. If you're rich, it meant God was blessing you. By contrast, if bad things happened to you, it was assumed that was because of your sins. Even Jesus' disciples thought this way, as John's gospel tells us: "As he [Jesus] went along, he saw a man blind from birth. His disciples asked him, 'Rabbi, who sinned, this man or his parents, that he was born blind?'"[178] Jesus sets them straight, saying neither the man's nor his parents' sins had anything to do with his condition.

The disciples were typical of their contemporaries in associating suffering with sin. People who thought that way also weren't seeing straight. They would have made the same wrong assumption as the self-satisfied Dives: that he was blessed by God, and that Lazarus was not. Nor did they grasp the unwelcome reality that, like Lazarus, we

---

[177] *African Bible Commentary*, p. 1237.
[178] John 9:1-2.

may go through life deprived of what the world sees as blessedness, a condition that may come only after the resurrection. For Christians are often called to a life of pain and suffering. Think of Jesus' command: "Whoever wants to be my disciple must deny themselves and take up their cross daily and follow me."[179] Then think of Jesus' life: one of impoverishment, with no place to call home, a journey of rejection by the powers that be, and ultimately an ignominious death on that very cross that told His followers to take on for themselves as the price of discipleship.

Back to Lazarus and the rich man. The parable is mostly about Dives; he has all the speaking lines, together with Abraham. Lazarus gets to say nothing. The parable is at least partly a warning against the seduction of wealth, and how it can insulate us from and numb us to our fellow human beings, like a Lazarus at our gate, or a homeless person sleeping rough under that main bridge downtown.

Beside avoiding the mistaken equation of *material blessing=God's favor*, we also need to recognize the equally inaccurate opposite: *an absence of material blessing=God's disfavor.* Job knew all about the removal of blessings, to the point where his life was a living hell. Yet never can we say, as he didn't either, that an absence of blessings means we've earned God's displeasure. For the God we serve operates in mysterious ways; He doesn't dispense blessings the way we might prefer. "The God of the Bible will not be domesticated. God comes to us on God's terms, not ours; when God chooses, not when we choose; in God's way, not our way. God reveals what God reveals. For all the certainty we seek, we get mystery."[180] Meanwhile, all we can do is ground our lives in the meaning of Lazarus' name, "God is my help."

---

[179] Luke 9:23.
[180] James Chatham, *Is it I, Lord?* p. 84.

44

Blessings as Booty

Wiktionary defines *booty* as "Something that has been stolen or illegally obtained from elsewhere." The website also refers to booty as plunder taken in war, or treasures taken from a seized ship. When it comes to God's blessings, we'll add a fourth take on the word: Hanging onto an undue portion of what God has given you.

The story is told of a Christian businessman who'd done extremely well. He was showing his pastor around his palatial six-bedroom home by the lake. The walls were decorated with high-end pieces of art, valued at well over half a million dollars. And in the three-car garage were cars each costing more than $75,000. The businessman told the pastor, "We're so blessed; God has given us so much." The pastor responded, "And how much did you need to keep?"

Compared with the developing world, most people in the United States, Canada, Europe and Japan, for example, live in great material comfort. We have access to good healthcare, decent housing, a high level of education for our children, and so on. Surely God wants all people to live healthy lives, with decent shelter and the opportunity to maximize their God-given potential. To the extent that we have these blessings, we should be grateful.

While we need to accept with gratitude these blessings God gives us, a problem arises when we as individuals and as societies take hold of more than we need. The blessings are then in danger of becoming like the manna that sustained the Israelites in the desert. Manna which was hoarded, contrary to Moses' direction, turned rotten: "… some of them paid no attention to Moses; they kept part of it until morning, but it was full of maggots and began to smell."[181]

This is a good place to mention the notion of the prosperity gospel, which according to historian Kate Bowler is "… a wildly popular Christian message of spiritual, physical, and financial mastery that dominates not only much of the American religious scene but some of the largest churches around the globe."[182] The prosperity gospel is a woefully misguided interpretation of God's blessings and a serious distortion of the gospel and its demands for sacrifice and the need to take up our cross in following Jesus. So much so that Andrew Davison commits a full chapter describing its importance in his book, *Blessing*.

So how should we approach our finances? Philip Yancey tells of a pastor he met who said Christians should ask themselves three questions about their money:

1. How did you get it? (Did it involve injustice, cheating, oppression of the poor?)
2. What are you doing with it? (Are you hoarding it? Exploiting others? Wasting it on needless luxuries?)
3. What is it doing to you?[183]

Questions 2 and 3 are especially pertinent to our focus on the "manna of money" for which Christians in the affluent West need to be accountable to God. J. Oswald Sanders put the issue of giving in perspective when he wrote, "The basic question is not how much of

---

[181] Exodus 16:20.
[182] Quoted in Andrew Davison, *Blessing*, p. 30.
[183] Philip Yancey, *Grace Notes*, p. 56.

our money we should give to God, but how much of God's money we should keep for ourselves."[184] Or to express that idea in terms of tithing, we need to consider that God doesn't expect us to give ten percent but that He allows us to keep ninety percent of our income.

It's one thing to be invited to a buffet table of God's blessings; it's another to pile our plate so high that we'll never eat it all.

---

[184] J. Oswald Sanders, *A Spiritual Clinic*, p. 85.

45

Inducing a Blessing

If you're an expectant mom and your baby's showing no signs of joining the human race any time soon, your doctor or midwife may well introduce you to Pitocin.[185] It's the brand name of a synthetic hormone, which mirrors the natural one you have in your body, oxytocin. Both serve to trigger contractions. So if you're one or two weeks overdue, or if you have a medical condition like high blood pressure or diabetes, or if there are concerns about the baby's wellbeing, you may be given Pitocin through your IV, in slowly increasing doses to get labor going.

Millions of women have benefited from the synthetic form, almost all of them no doubt unaware of the meaning of the natural hormone: oxytocin, not to be confused with oxycontin, the highly addictive pain killer. Oxytocin is made up of two Greek words meaning *quick birth*. And a quick and healthy birth is what we wish for all expectant moms.

But many of us have wished there were some kind of divine version of Pitocin, that we could give God to hurry things along. When we read in Revelation that He promises to "make all things new,"[186] we often find ourselves saying, "But *when?*"

To be sure, we're fully confident that this assurance of "all things new" can only be good; God's character and track record are that He

---

[185] This entry is adapted from Gordon S. Jackson, *Ninety Days of Difference*.
[186] Revelation 21:5 (*King James Version*).

seeks to bless us in one way after another. Maybe it's a particular blessing we're seeking: a new job that will take us from our current toxic work situation, or a desire to get pregnant and begin a family in spite of the difficulties your doctor has identified. Or perhaps it's a combination of circumstances that are making life miserable right now. You say to yourself, "Life is just plain crappy, Lord; where is that blessed life you promised? When will things get better?" Or like a woman struggling through difficult labor, you desperately wish the blessing of a new birth would come sooner rather than later.

You may be tempted to give up, despair or engage in angry rants against God for not changing your circumstances for the better. Whatever your situation, it's time to heed the advice of two individuals. One is James, who writes in his epistle: "Blessed is the one who perseveres under trial because, having stood the test, that person will receive the crown of life that the Lord has promised to those who love him."[187]

The other person worth hearing is Stephen Merritt, who warned: "Cease meddling with God's plans and will. You touch anything of His and you mar the work. You may move the hands of a clock, but you do not change the time; so you may hurry the unfolding of God's will, but you harm and may not help the work."[188]

The apostle Peter points to the gap between our handle on time and that of the One who transcends time as we know it: "With the Lord a day is like a thousand years, and a thousand years are like a day."[189] In ways we cannot conceive, He is able and willing to endure an unimaginably long labor to bring those "new things" into being, to match His perfect timing. And He does so without our offer of Pitocin.

It's been said that God is never in a hurry, but He's never late. Nor are His blessings.

---

[187] James 1:12.
[188] Quoted in *Streams in the Desert*, March 30.
[189] 2 Peter 3:8.

46

Blessings Gone AWOL?

I have never found anyone so religious and devout that he did not sometimes feel grace withdrawn and his favor lessened.
—*Thomas à Kempis,* The Imitation of Christ[190]

Sometimes life is just crappy. Even the Christian life. You may have had a lousy day at work or school. Your teenage daughter may have been more insolent than usual. Or you're struggling with long COVID, and the fatigue just won't go away. In short, you're no longer counting your blessings; you're wondering where they went. Oh, you recognize that in the big picture God is still in control. But it certainly doesn't feel like that today. Instead, it seems God has withdrawn His grace and "lessened his favor," to quote à Kempis.

But elsewhere in his classic devotional, à Kempis imagines the Lord speaking, "My son, you must not rely on how you feel at the moment, for you will soon feel something quite different."[191] If you're steeped in the language of the *King James Bible,* you might even have told yourself, despite à Kempis' warning, "Woe is me." Perversely, your feelings kept spiraling you downwards; you found yourself down in the dumps and just kept descending....

Time out for a reality check about feelings. Eugene Peterson puts it quite bluntly: "Feelings are great liars." He adds: "Feelings are

---

[190] Thomas à Kempis, *The Imitation of Christ*, translated by Betty Knott, p. 98.
[191] Thomas à Kempis, *The Imitation of Christ*, translated by Betty Knott, p. 163.

important in many areas but completely unreliable in matters of faith." He quotes Paul Scherer as saying that "The Bible wastes very little time on the way we feel."[192] And F. B. Meyer, in *The Secret of Guidance*, writes: "Our feelings are very deceptive.... They are affected by the state of our health, changes in the weather, the society or absence of those we love."[193]

It's time to reframe your situation and focus instead on your identity. You are a child of God, serving in Kingdom work. You are also human and may have unwittingly made some kind of mistake that led to your unhappiness. Or maybe you were the victim of a colleague's unwarranted nastiness that you should have shrugged off but can't. Or it could be that you're in a slump spiritually. Whatever the reason, none of this detracts from your identity, which includes your being God's person, in God's place, at God's time. You are not in your current station in life by chance or coincidence. How you *feel* today is ultimately unimportant.

There's nothing wrong with having deep feelings. Perhaps you are by nature someone whose emotions are close to the surface. You serve a feeling Lord, who Himself wept on learning of Lazarus' death; over Jerusalem; and in the Garden of Gethsemane. But we know too that those feelings never let Jesus be distracted from His mission. He was always clear on who He was and what He was called to do.

Where does that leave you? Still feeling crappy, perhaps. But don't let your feelings threaten to undercut your identity or eat away at your Christian commitment. If you're down in the dumps and feel "blessing-deprived" or "blessing-challenged," remind yourself of the wisdom captured in two hymns. This first is John Newton's *Amazing Grace*: "The Lord has promised good to me, his word my hope secures...." Then there is the line from a Fanny Crosby hymn, "Blessed assurance, Jesus is mine; Oh, what a foretaste of glory divine!"

These words help you to focus on the blessings that you *know* are there. Write down these lyrics, perhaps. Or say aloud to yourself, "I am

---

[192] Quoted in Gordon S. Jackson, *A Handbook for Discovering God's Will*, p. 59.
[193] Quoted in Gordon S. Jackson, *A Handbook for Discovering God's Will*, p. 59.

blessed, I am blessed, I am blessed." Keep saying it until you believe it. And if your slump is deep enough, remember the words of Matthew Henry, who said: "Whatever low or darksome valley we are called into at any time, we may be confident, if God go down with us into it, that he will surely bring us up again."[194] That promise should be blessing enough.

---

[194] *Matthew Henry's Commentary* (1 volume), p. 66.

47

Blessings for the Undeserving

[Y]our Father in heaven ... causes his sun to rise on the evil and the good,
and sends rain on the righteous and the unrighteous.
                    —Matthew 5:45

The Lord is good to all; he has compassion on all he has made.
                    —Psalm 145:9

"Not fair," we say. Why do we, who seek to follow Jesus, see those who are not entitled to benefit from the blessings of sunshine and rain, and everything else in life? Fortunately, Jesus himself anticipated our question, so He told the parable of the laborers chosen for work at different times of the day.[195] Then, when the owner of the vineyard came to pay the workers, those who showed up last got the same as the first hired—and the charge of unfairness arose. The owner responded, "I am not being unfair to you, friend. Didn't you agree to work for a denarius? Take your pay and go. I want to give the one who was hired last the same as I gave you. Don't I have the right to do what I want with my own money? Or are you envious because I am generous?"[196]

We're not talking about evil workers who defrauded the owner; they were fellow laborers who were, on the face of it, way overpaid for their labor. By any economic standards, the longer-serving workers had

---

[195] Matthew 20.
[196] Matthew 20:13-15.

good reason to expect more than those they justifiably saw as Johnny-come-latelies.

But the parable isn't about equal pay for equal work. Instead, it's about a lavish, generous God who knows the last arrivals are in as much need of a day's wage to feed their families. It's an uncomfortable lesson for those longer-serving workers, for the owner is right on target when he accuses them of being envious of their fellow laborers. The latecomers valued the blessing of a day's wage all the more because they thought they'd go the whole day without pay. The owner's generosity ensured they did not.

What about us? Do we find ourselves resenting God's generosity, which entails blessings falling on people who we *know* for a fact don't deserve them? "Not fair," we cry....

Time out for a reality check. We think we are so special that we are entitled to God's blessing, while others are not? Or, at least, no more than we got? We should instead be rejoicing with our friends and neighbors who got employed at the last minute.

To draw on another of Jesus' parables,[197] it's as if I'm in a debtors' court when a billionaire comes and pays off my debt of $100,000. I'm unbelievably happy—until I learn he's also paid off the debts of someone owing $1,000,000. I feel cheated, like a 4-year-old, because his blessing is bigger than mine. I've taken my eyes off the source of my blessing, this generous God, and focused instead on the subject of my envy and resentment. God's likely response? Probably to tell me that it's past time to stop acting and thinking like a 4-year-old.

---

[197] Matthew 18:23-34.

48

Blessings Bearing Bad Fruit

We understandably assume that good things should lead to other good things. Take education, for example. We'd expect that even a rudimentary education that enabled one to read and write to be a blessing to that individual. We'd also expect it to be a blessing to the society as a whole. All the more so, then, should we expect advanced education to be a blessing to our communities, our society and our culture. We need doctors and nurses, lawyers, engineers, architects, and economists. All those people play invaluable roles in enriching our societies, as well as benefiting us as individuals.

"I was so blessed during my back surgery to have a wonderful team of doctors and nurses; they were all great." Or, "We were so blessed to have Mr. Kingston as our lawyer, steering us through the mess of Mom's estate." Think of the time someone else's education was a blessing to you, whether you realized it or not.

But advanced education does not always bear the fruit we would hope, and to which as a society, we are entitled after investing in its recipients. The historian, Antony Beevor, tells how in World War II, a group of senior German officials met in Berlin on January 20, 1940. Reinhard Heydrich, the deputy head of the SS under Heinrich Himmler, led the meeting, at which another official arrived with a chilling document: "… a carefully prepared memorandum entitled 'Requests and Ideas of the Foreign Ministry in Connection with the Intended Final Solution of the Jewish Question in Europe.'" Then

Beevor adds, "Just over half those present had doctorates, and a significant minority were lawyers."[198] So much brain power, yet so much evil in a single room.

The fact that we or others have been blessed with education or other good things comes with no guarantees that these blessings will bear good fruit. Skilled political leaders may betray their oath of office. Or others may betray the gifts entrusted to them. The legendary news anchor, Walter Cronkite, once bumped into a former protégé of his, a young man blessed with considerable talent, who had left the CBS network and took that talent to a sleazy tabloid show. Cronkite asked him, "I had no idea you had fallen so far. Do they pay you well?"

Then there's the dramatized example in the story of Sir Thomas More, told in Robert Bolt's play, *A Man for All Seasons*. The film version culminates with Sir Thomas on trial for treason, for which he is found guilty based on the perjured evidence of Richard Rich—a gifted but ruthless politician. More knows he is doomed, based on Rich's lie. As Rich leaves the witness box, More notices he is wearing a chain of office. He asks him about it and Rich tells him it signifies he has been appointed attorney-general for Wales. Then comes More's scathing put-down: "For Wales? Why Richard, it profits a man nothing to give his soul for the whole world ... but for Wales!"

What good, in other words, are the blessings of skill or learning if you'll sell your soul and betray your God-given gifts or opportunities?

---

[198] Antony Beevor, *The Second World War*, p. 294.

49

Blindness—A Blessing?

S urely not.

Well, not if you listen to John Hull, a blind theologian.[199] Hull was a professor of religious education at the University of Birmingham in England. Originally from Australia, he developed serious vision problems in his teens and later became totally blind. He begins his book, *In the Beginning There Was Darkness*, by spelling out the tension that he and other blind Christians face upon encountering the Bible. His difficulty starts at the beginning of Genesis:

> *"And God saw that the light was good" (Genesis 1:4). Now we know what we have suspected throughout this passage [Genesis 1 onwards]: God is not on the side of blind people. God pronounces as good something that means nothing to those who are totally blind, and that is a source of longing and frustration, perhaps even despair, for those who still have a little sight. Here we come upon one of the great stumbling blocks that the Bible places in the way of blind people. It speaks of values that, for them, cannot be values. It announces that God is on the side of, and has a preference for, a world that is not their world—a reality to which they have no access.[200]*

---

[199] This section is excerpted in part from Gordon S. Jackson, *Be Thou My Vision: Light, Sight and the Christian Faith.*

[200] Hull, *In the Beginning*, p. 2.

This is strong stuff. But on the next page, his view softens: "I now realize that my first thought—that God is not on the side of the blind—was too hasty." Reflecting on God's creation of the darkness as well as the light, he continues, "God is the One who broods over blindness, calling it out of shapelessness and confusion, giving it a place of beauty and order in the fullness of creation. God blesses blindness and hallows it."[201]

He then provides a series of case studies of blindness in the Old and New Testaments, as he considers what we can learn from a nearly blind Isaac and his deceiving son Jacob, Samson's blinding, and King Zedekiah, which he says represents the final blindness of the monarchy. In the New Testament, he analyzes Jesus' various healings of blind people. Hull's insights are all the richer, coming from the perspective of someone who is himself blind.

Although he moves beyond the harshness of his initial responses quoted above, Hull returns repeatedly to the difficulty blind people have with the images of light and sight that occur throughout Scripture. He notes for example how, after he went blind, re-reading the gospel of John was particularly difficult. It was the first book he read in Braille and, he says, "I was delighted to have access once again to so many familiar and greatly loved passages. However, the symbolism made me feel uneasy and I soon came to realize that this book was not written for people like me but for sighted people. No other book in the Bible is so dominated by the contrast between light and darkness, and blindness is a symbol of darkness."[202]

And yet, as we noted above, Hull said, "God blesses blindness and hallows it." His reconciliation with his blindness parallels Paul's experience and his description of his "thorn in the flesh:

> *...in order to keep me from becoming conceited, I was given a thorn in my flesh, a messenger of Satan, to torment me. Three times I pleaded with the Lord to take it away from me. But he said to me, 'My grace is sufficient for you, for my power is made perfect in weakness." Therefore I will boast all the more gladly about my weaknesses, so that Christ's power may rest on*

---

[201] Hull, *In the Beginning*, p. 3.
[202] Hull, *In the Beginning*, pp. 49-50.

me. That is why, for Christ's sake, I delight in weaknesses, in insults, in hardships, in persecutions, in difficulties. For when I am weak, then I am strong.[203]

It is not self-deluding thinking that led men like John Hull and Paul the Apostle to transform a thorn into a positive blessing. They were given the insight and wisdom to grasp a bigger picture of God's work in their lives.

Then there are those of us who take the blessing of sight for granted, as captured by the Welsh poet Huw Menai:

If the good God were suddenly
To make a solitary Blind to see
We would stand wondering all
And call it a miracle;
But that he gives with lavish hand
Sight to a million souls we stand
And say, with little awe,
He but fulfills a natural law.

The gift of sight is an obvious blessing. But blindness too? With God's grace and power, and not without deep struggle, the amazing answer can be an unexpected "yes."

---

[203] 2 Corinthians 12:7-10.

PART 5

Concluding Matters

50

Saying Goodbye—Benedictions and Doxologies

Doxologies are blessings at the end of a church service or some other religious event. Let us conclude with three familiar "godly sign-offs." The first is the fuller version of the familiar and beloved blessing cited in the **Introduction**, by Thomas Ken:

Praise God from whom all blessings flow,
Praise Him, all creatures here below,
Praise Him above, ye heavenly host,
Praise Father, Son, and Holy Ghost.

The second is from the 1928 version of *The Book of Common Prayer*. This version, with its now-dated language is worth keeping to honor those millions who grew up with this wording, from which they'd derive great benefit as they were dismissed from worship each week. (Feel free, if you'd prefer, to replace *passeth* with *passes* and use *Holy Spirit* instead of *Holy Ghost*.)

The peace of God, which passeth all understanding, keep your hearts and minds in the knowledge and love of God, and of his Son Jesus Christ our Lord: And the blessing of God Almighty, the Father, the Son, and the Holy Ghost, be amongst you and remain with you always. Amen.

Finally, let's turn to the magnificent conclusion of Jude's epistle, paying special attention to Jesus' readiness to keep us from stumbling as we journey on with Him, and to the corollary that as a result, we will appear in His presence without fault.

> *To him who is able to keep you from stumbling and to present you before his glorious presence without fault and with great joy—to the only God our Savior be glory, majesty, power and authority, through Jesus Christ our Lord, before all ages, now and forevermore! Amen.*[204]

The function of a blessing at the end of a church service is not merely to say "all done; let's head to the fellowship hall." Rather, it orients us to what's next. We need to focus now on what God expects next, as we re-engage the world around us. Many churches have something like this saying posted over the exits from the sanctuary: "You are now entering your mission field." Ideally, we should have been spiritually fed and thus equipped for this new week's journey. The blessing given at the end of the service is in effect saying, "Go now about God's business this week, knowing that you are in His hands and that nothing can happen to you without His knowledge; be aware of His blessings that will sustain you this week; and seek whatever opportunities you can to advance God's Kingdom. Ready? Now go."

---

[204] Jude 24-25.

Afterword

We began with Andrew Davison's words in the epigraph, "Christ's last act before his ascension was to bless his disciples...."[205] And that is how we will finish. For all our talk about hallowed and colloquial blessings, who gets to bless, and case studies of Saul and Pharaoh, we need to return to that last action of Jesus—for two reasons. The first is to recognize the importance of blessing. Of all the things Jesus could have done, He chose to bless His disciples. He could have given them some final instructions. He could have shared with them some kind of Transfiguration experience. Instead, He blessed them.

The second reason was that Jesus' blessing, by definition, anchored their future in a God-initiated ministry, empowering and equipping them to preach the good news of the gospel. That blessing echoes down through the centuries and sustains all of us who today call ourselves Christians.

And so we finish this survey, aware that it is incomplete, with various topics under-explored, and possibly others that you hoped would be addressed not touched on at all. But it is hoped that these reflections have helped you better understand the nature of blessing and what it means to be in a state of blessedness, as we get glimpses in our earthly existence of what God's **Shalom** looks like. They are only glimpses, because whether through our limitations or hesitation in asking, we enjoy only a little of what God offers us. Benjamin Jowett wrote, "What have I asked for? I have asked for a cupful, and the ocean remains! I have asked for a sunbeam, and the sun abides. My

---

[205] Andrew Davison, *Blessing,* p. 3.

best asking falls immeasurably short of my father's giving: it is beyond what we can ask."[206]

We are to move forward then with profound gratitude for the blessings in which we are immersed, so many of which we don't even recognize. But overriding everything is our anticipation of that Ultimate Blessing: of eternity, spent with the God who blesses.

---

[206] Quoted in *Streams in the Desert*, July 27.

Acknowledgements

My thanks to those individuals who have strengthened earlier drafts of book with their insights and probing questions, or via their thoughtful conversations about the nature of blessings. They include the Rev. Carl Green, Jeff Haschick, Fr Pat Kerst, Prof. Josh Leim, Lisa McLean and, sadly, the late Marjorie Peters.

More generally, I am deeply indebted to those writers who shaped my thinking on the topic of blessings; their ideas and wisdom are evident throughout this volume.

About Kharis Publishing:

Kharis Publishing, an imprint of Kharis Media LLC, is a leading Christian and inspirational book publisher based in Aurora, Chicago metropolitan area, Illinois. Kharis' dual mission is to give voice to under-represented writers (including women and first-time authors) and equip orphans in developing countries with literacy tools. That is why, for each book sold, the publisher channels some of the proceeds into providing books and computers for orphanages in developing countries so that these kids may learn to read, dream, and grow. For a limited time, Kharis Publishing is accepting unsolicited queries for nonfiction (Christian, self-help, memoirs, business, health and wellness) from qualified leaders, professionals, pastors, and ministers. Learn more at: About Us - Kharis Publishing - Accepting Manuscript